The 4 Es of Entrepreneurship: Exposure, Economics, Environment, and Execution

The 4 Es of Entrepreneurship: Exposure, Economics, Environment, and Execution

A COLLECTION OF COACHING SESSIONS FOR ENTREPRENEURS THAT LEAD TO RESULTS OVER AND OVER AGAIN.

Roddric W. Sims

To Nokhomas Sims-Stanley, my mother and first example of work ethic and dedication, you may not have known it all those years, but I was watching.

And to Roddric Donovan and Ryan Dillon, my sons and reasons for my focused work ethic and dedication, you may not have known, but I always will be on your team and will always be watching.

I really believed my plan was foolproof and concrete until Roddric Sims and the Sims Coaching Group offered me exactly what I needed. And through very thought-provoking sessions, I realized I hadn't covered all my bases, nor did I consider all the possible options. Every entrepreneur should enlist the services of a business coach.

No matter how sound of a plan you may have, the problem could be in the execution or just simply lack of consideration of the small things often looked over that hinder progress. The businesses that employ coaching as a part of their planning strategy will be the champions of the future. After all, what would Michael Jordan and the Bulls have been without Phil Jackson?

Arthur Muhammad
Original Man's Barber & Style Shop

Roddric Sims of Sims Coaching Group really gave me and my business the direction that I needed to get off to a great start. He consulted with me when I was just beginning and gathering my thoughts around how to set up my company. He gave me an assignment and had me turn it in, which was great! It gave me the focus that I needed and allowed me to think through various aspects of running a successful company. I can truly say that without Roddric, my company would have gotten off to a much slower start and would not have been as organized as it could have been. I truly appreciate him and his advice. Keep up the great work!

Nickqoulette Barrett
IRock Resume Services

I'm extremely impressed with the quality coaching offered by the Sims Coaching Group. Mr. Sims made going over my business plan a painless process. He has a gift, not only for being a good listener, but also for providing a very studied analysis of what he's heard. As a result, his coaching style included vital questions that helped me to uncover my own road blocks. With road-blocks revealed, he then encouraged me to explore solutions that fit my work style! Highly recommended!
Rushia Butler, MD
Wellness Integrative Services

Roddric was attentive, thoughtful, and objective in helping me to make a key business decision. He provided options rather than pushy advice and assisted me in analyzing my decisions within the context of a five-year plan for my business. Through our coaching session, I gained the confidence and clarity to take my business to the next level.
Ebony Wilkerson
Attorney-at-Law
Peace of Mind, LLC

Roddric Sims and the Sims Coaching Group is a great resource for the entrepreneur who wants to take it to the next level and then to the next. He is a catalyst for entrepreneurs who want to surpass their goals. He helps create systems, processes, and tangible goals for the entrepreneur to excel. With over 10 very successful years

of coaching entrepreneurs to surpass their dreams, I am glad he is on my team.
Janet W. Thomas
Winning Consultants

Contents

Introduction

This book is for anyone interested in entrepreneurship at any stage of his or her business but will probably resonate more with those who are aspiring to be entrepreneurs. In my ten plus years of coaching entrepreneurs, I have worked with over two thousand aspiring entrepreneurs in one-on-one or in group coaching sessions and have seen hundreds of them go on to launch their own small businesses. During this time, I have always been amazed by how many plan to start their businesses without really understanding what it will take to start, grow, and sell them. My belief is this is truly one of the main reasons that greater than 50 percent of small businesses fail before they have made it to the five-year mark.

Now, for clarity, this book might not save you from opening a business that fails. The intent is to create opportunities to go through several coaching conversations that I have had with clients over the years, which have led to results over and over again. And when I say results, I mean creating "aha" moments that lead to action or shifts in mind-set. The timing of these actions or shifts is what is critical to the long-term success of any business. Also, these clients are appreciative of the time and money I have saved them by helping them identify challenges and create action plans to overcome them and acting as their accountability partner.

And as I stepped back and looked at these conversations, I saw that they all tended to fall into one of four areas: exposure, economics, environment, and execution, which are actually the four sections of this book, *The 4 Es of Entrepreneurship*. Exposure to entrepreneurship is important, as it will help you set proper expectations. Understanding the economics of entrepreneurship will prepare you for the investment required. Researching the environment will let you know if the seeds of entrepreneurship you plant will actually grow. And last but not least, taking ownership of the fact that nothing else matters more to an entrepreneur's success than proper execution.

Even though this book has been organized in what I feel is the order that each section impacts the success time line of any entrepreneur, it can be read in any order, as each section stands on its own. Actually, each coaching session is listed as its own independent lesson, so the coaching sessions can be read in any order as well. I actually recommend this way; in most cases, each person is at different steps on his or her entrepreneurial journey, and any effective coaching session takes place based on the client's need.

Also, at the end of each section is a "Session Takeaways" worksheet that will allow you to recap what you have read into a summary section. It will also help to direct actions so that the coaching session does not end with this book. It will help turn my philosophy and experience into practical applications for you over and over again.

If you are ready for the first session, I know I am. Ready! Set! Let's go! (Sorry, I couldn't help myself right there. I am a coach.)

Section One

The 1st E of Entrepreneurship— Exposure

Exposure[1]

- the fact or condition of being affected by something or experiencing something: the condition of being exposed *to* something
- the act of revealing secrets about someone or something
- public attention and notice

---

1 *Merriam-Webster*, s.v. "Exposure," accessed July, 10 2016, http://www.merriam-webster.com/dictionary/exposure.

COACHING SESSION 1

An Entrepreneur's Nightmare

> If you've got an idea, start today. There's
> no better time than now to get going.
> That doesn't mean quit your job and
> jump into your idea 100 percent from
> day one, but there's always small progress
> that can be made to start the movement.
> —KEVIN SYSTROM, FOUNDER OF INSTAGRAM

As a coach to entrepreneurs for over ten years, I have become accustomed to hearing many of the highs and lows that take place during the cycle of business ownership, from the excitement of that grand opening and making the first sale to the despair that takes place when realization sets in that the business is not going to make it. Since the success rate for most new businesses after five years is less than 50 percent, I often have to be the one to make my clients aware that there is as much chance they will fail as they will succeed.

My intent is not to scare them away from taking the risk of owning their own business but to provide the perspective that, if not done right, the decision to take the entrepreneurial path can be one of the most impactful decisions an entrepreneur will ever make and can have lifelong implications. I accomplish this by telling aspiring entrepreneurs this short story that might give them nightmares.

During a long commute home from an even longer day at work, John decides, "That's it! I am going to go ahead and start that business!" which he has been thinking about for the last six months. With that, he marches home and tells his wife all about this great idea, how everyone else is doing it, and how it will be life changing for the family. For a while, she is hesitant, but after a great sales job over a few weeks, he convinces her that there is no way he could fail and that they can't afford to wait any longer. She buys in and jumps on the bandwagon as well. The dream of being a business owner begins...

Now, we fast-forward a couple of years ahead, and things are not going well. The business is on the brink of closing, his wife has filed for divorce, and our aspiring entrepreneur's bank accounts are close to zero! "What went wrong?" you ask. Well, to be honest, a lot of things that could have been avoided. Let's take a look at how this nightmare came to be.

When the business was launched, it was done on a whim. John did not do any real research and neglected to complete his business plan. He was right that everyone was opening that type of business, but what he neglected to realize was that the number of people in the business made it hard to charge a lot for his service and that the profit margins were really small. So even though he is making enough money to keep the doors open, he is not making the money he thought he would. He is actually making less and working harder than he did at the job he left, even though he has been open three years. The fact that he is making less money and working more hours has him considering closing the business and going back to his old company. The good news is that they are willing to hire him back, but the bad news is that it is not at the level he was before. The role he had worked fifteen years to obtain was filled soon after he left.

As far as the divorce is concerned, the business has put a huge amount of stress on his spouse. When he sold his wife on the business, he neglected to share with her that the first few years would be quite challenging for everyone. Now that he has to work more hours at the business, he is around a lot less than before, and his wife has had to step up and do more things around the house, explain to the children why their dad no longer makes it to their events, and shop differently as their income is substantially less than it was before. Even though these things are not unusual for a new business owner, the wife has stated over and over again she would not have agreed so easily if he had told her the truth. She feels as though she was tricked, and now the whole family is paying the price.

And, last but not least, there are the bank accounts. In order to open a business, the majority of time, the start-up capital will come from the entrepreneur's own personal savings and investments. This case is not different. In order to open the business, John used all of the family's savings. He knew it would take some money but did not realize it would be so much. After using his savings to open the business, he had to deal with the fact that the business took six months before it broke even, and there was a need to support it and the family. In order to do this, it was necessary to cash out the money they had invested in the stock market and tap into their retirement funds. This also magnified the strong feeling of betrayal that his wife had begun feeling once the business launched.

So, in recap, three years later, John is potentially returning to the job he had left at a lower salary. He has spent his savings and cashed in all of his investments. Plus, his marriage is on the rocks, and divorce is looming in the horizon. Sounds like a nightmare to me! Unfortunately, this reality and worse takes place as often as not.

Now, when I share this story with potential clients or an aspiring entrepreneur in general, some ask if I am trying to scare them away from being business owners. Of course, I am not! But honestly, if my nightmare keeps them from starting businesses they are either risk averse, realize that they have not planned correctly, or have not had the right conversation with their families. If any of these are true, I have just saved them from creating their own nightmare. And creating their own nightmare is something that I am trying to scare them away from!

Session Review Question: Have you set realistic expectations of what challenges you may experience as an entrepreneur?

COACHING SESSION 2

Are You More of a Business Owner or an Entrepreneur?

> Business opportunities are like buses:
> there's always another one coming.
> —RICHARD BRANSON, CHAIRMAN
> AND FOUNDER OF VIRGIN GROUP

Over the years, I have noticed there is a difference between being a business owner and being an entrepreneur. Even though having entrepreneurial spirit is a significant component of owning a business, it is not the only one. And being a great business owner does not necessarily make you a great entrepreneur.

If you agree with the philosophy that "entrepreneurship is about creating streams of income," then a business that has significant time demands could limit the creativity that many entrepreneurs need to travel several paths at the same time. Many entrepreneurs get bored after a few years in the same business and seek to move on to new endeavors. These "serial" entrepreneurs are always seeking to create the next big idea. For example, franchising does not always work for them, as they enjoy creating the business completely from scratch. If this sounds like you, here are a few things you can do to position yourself properly.

- **Build your business with the intent that you could walk away from it.** This does not mean to build a bad business. But do not get too emotionally attached. When that next great opportunity comes up, you will want to be able to run to it.
- **Create a business that can be sold.** The amount of time and energy that you will put into any successful business will be hard to run from unless you have a return on your investment (ROI). This ROI could be the seed money for that next big venture.
- **Consider bringing in a business partner from the beginning.** This business partner might be able to take over the business when your attention is diverted or may even be in a position to buy you out if you do decide to completely leave. Since the partner was there from the development or initial phases, he or she could be as invested as you.

Great business owners tend to be a little more conservative than the "serial" entrepreneur. They prefer the idea of being in charge of a business for the long term versus creating a whole new business model. They get enjoyment from growing a business, managing employees, and opening multiple locations. A franchise opportunity is a great idea for them because they do not have to worry about creating everything and can focus on growing the business. Even great business owners should keep their eyes open for the following items as they grow their ventures.

- **Do your research!** Not all businesses are created the same. Make sure any opportunity you take on provides you with the level of support you need. Even though the level of support may be relative, the reason you are buying in is for a proven business model that *you* can readily implement.
- **Recognize the limitations.** Make sure there is the flexibility that you need to grow the business. Some owners are quite sensitive about their brand and will limit your ability to be creative or to change certain work processes and where you can do business.
- **Understand the commitment.** Since you are buying into this business, make sure this is something that you can see yourself doing for at least the next five years. The reason being is that it takes most business owners five years to break even. If you close or sell your business prior to that time, you will have a hard time generating the ROI that you planned.

Any entrepreneur, regardless of personality, needs to make an honest evaluation of why he or she wants to go into a business. Once completed, this evaluation will help build a business that positions the entrepreneur to be as successful as possible. At the end of the day, there is no one perfect business for all entrepreneurs, but there is always a perfect business out there for each entrepreneur.

Session Review Question: Is the opportunity to design your own business or the security of a proven business model more important to you?

COACHING SESSION 3

So You Want to Be an Entrepreneur? Do You Really Have What It Takes?

> I'm convinced that about half
> of what separates the successful
> entrepreneurs from the non-successful
> ones is pure perseverance.
> —STEVE JOBS, COFOUNDER OF APPLE

It takes a special person to be an entrepreneur. Unfortunately, not everyone has what it takes to be successful; that is why there are more employees than entrepreneurs. Entrepreneurs must possess a certain set of characteristics. Discipline, confidence, competitiveness, determination, and passion are all traits that entrepreneurs need in order to succeed. Lacking one of these traits could result in a business not being as successful as what was envisioned. Let's look at these characteristics a little more closely:

- **Discipline**—All entrepreneurs are creative; the challenge is to be disciplined enough to manage all the other parts of the business. Being able to manage multiple aspects of business and staying on plan is critical to small business success. Distractions will be abundant!
- **Confidence**—Entrepreneurs need to believe in themselves even when others don't. There will be many detractors and challenging situations that they will have to overcome.
- **Competitiveness**—In most cases, when a business is started, there will be a need to compete with other entrepreneurs in your industry. Increasing your competitive advantage will increase your chances for success.
- **Determination**—Part of being an entrepreneur is having the desire to assume risk *and* then being able to deal with the unforeseen outcomes of this risk. Staying focused on the vision even though there are roadblocks is mandatory.
- **Passion**—There will be no one around to make an entrepreneur do the hard things required. No one will ever have the same desire or, in most cases, as much invested for the endeavor to be successful.

In conjunction with the referenced internal characteristics, entrepreneurs must have strong social skills and understand how to interact with their employees, business partners, and customers. The abilities to communicate, lead, and influence stand out as a foundation for success in this area.

- **Communication**—Simply put, if an entrepreneur cannot communicate well, he or she will not effectively sell the business, product, or service to anyone.
- **Leadership**—Entrepreneurs have to be able to share their vision and drive results through others. If an employee does not feel welcomed or feels as if he or she is not having any impact on the company, it could discourage the employee and cause him or her go in the wrong direction and be less efficient.
- **Influence**—This skill is not only important to leading employees; it is also vital to being able to sell the vision of the business to potential investors, products or services to the customer base, and to convince the customer to provide referrals of friends and family so that the business can continue to grow.

It is not an easy journey on the road of entrepreneurship. Over time, the endeavor may run into a lot of bumps in the road and setbacks, but the role of the entrepreneur is to adjust whichever way needed to continue bringing in revenue. It takes a strong-willed person to defy the odds and build a profitable business. If you have the skills and characteristics discussed, you may just have what it takes to be that next success story that other aspiring entrepreneurs admire.

Session Review Questions: What is the one characteristic you will excel at and the one characteristic that will challenge you daily as an entrepreneur?

COACHING SESSION 4

Starting a Business Is Like Raising a Child!

> You don't learn to walk by following
> rules. You learn by doing and falling over.
> —RICHARD BRANSON, FOUNDER
> OF VIRGIN GROUP

During an entrepreneurship workshop that I led a few years ago, one of the current business owners raised her hand and surprised a lot of the aspiring business owners when she stated, "I have not worked this hard since my son was a baby!" Even though it might be hard for some to believe, this statement makes a lot of sense when you think of how a small business develops over time. Let me show you how and see if you agree.

When a child is born, you have to be with him or her twenty-four hours a day seven days a week, as the infant cannot take care of him- or herself at all. Now, even though a small business is not living and breathing, it still has to be taken care of by its owner around the clock when it is first "born" or opened. Typically as a small business owner, you are not only the CEO but also the head cashier, stock clerk, and even janitor at times when you first start out. When something happens at the office after hours, guess who will get the call and have to get out of a warm, comfortable bed to go in and check on things. Sounds just like what happens to a parent when a baby starts crying in the middle of the night, doesn't it?

Now, don't panic! As a child grows up, a parent does not have to spend all of the time he or she did when the child was young. By the time the child is a toddler, he or she can do a few things on his or her own, and so will a new business. As the business grows, more revenue is generated, and it can begin taking care of itself a little bit more, as now the owner can hire others to do some of the things that needed to be done by him or her during its infancy. Also, the owner now has established work processes that help the business run. This allows the business owner to get a full night of sleep as the business now "sleeps through the night."

As we fast-forward to the teenage years, your child has become very independent and can do a lot for him- or herself. He or she has grown and now created his or her own identity but still needs significant support from the parents. Hopefully, a business owner will have the opportunity to see the business mature to this point. This is the period where the business may "run itself," but the owner has to continue to check in on it to make sure that it is on the right path. This happens by making sure the business is developing properly and has not lost its focus on profitability. There may even be a time when the direction of the business may need to change to keep up with the times. Now, the business owner can take those well-deserved vacations and leave the "child" at home by itself.

Finally, the child becomes an adult and strikes out on his or her own. Instead of seeing the parents daily, the child moves out and comes home to visit on the holidays, which in a lot of cases is a parent's ultimate fantasy. No longer does the child need your help, but he or she may rely on you as more of a consultant that he or she reaches out to when necessary. As for the business owner, the business is now at a similar stage. It now only needs to be checked on, and the owner does not have to be around for it to grow. At this stage is when a business can be expanded or even franchised. It is financially independent and has a proven track record of success that can be shared with others who want to become "parents." And of course, the business owner has time for this now because the business that he or she started originally now has a "life of its own."

Even though it is hard to debate that there is nothing more rewarding than to see a child grow into an adult, I have met several entrepreneurs who have received a similar sense of satisfaction by starting and growing their own businesses. Since the two share so many similarities, can you really blame them? Either way, it was hard work raising that "child."

Session Review Question: What stage of childhood is your business idea in?

COACHING SESSION 5

Entrepreneurship Is about Risk! Sacrifice! Achievement!

> If you're not a risk taker, you should
> get the hell out of business.
> —RAY KROC, FOUNDER OF MCDONALD'S

Are you strongly considering taking the leap into entrepreneurship? If so, then let's make sure that you know the three fundamental things that entrepreneurship is about before you get started.

1. **Entrepreneurship is about *risk*!** As an entrepreneur, you face an inherent risk that can't be avoided. If you are looking for a steady income, a guaranteed ROI, and a greater than 50 percent chance for success, then you might not be going down the right path. The majority of entrepreneurs fail during their first journey into this world. This reality is not something to fear or to

stop you from jumping in with both feet, but you need to be aware of it so that you make the best decisions possible before you launch. And if failure is the outcome, then there should be a significant number of takeaways that you will have learned that you can use during your next try.

2. **Entrepreneurship is about *sacrifice*!** To be as successful as possible as an entrepreneur, you will need to make several sacrifices. Some of the main sacrifices are of time and money. In order to get your business up and running, you will need investment capital. For the majority of small business owners, this means they will need to tap into their personal savings. Along with that, there is a strong potential that it might take you two to three years for your business to break even, meaning you have made back the money from your original investment. This means making less money in the short term so that you make more in the long term. As for the sacrifice of time, an entrepreneur will typically have to work harder for himself or herself than he or she would for anyone else. This may mean longer hours or more stress, depending of the size and the industry of your business.

3. **Entrepreneurship is about *achievement*!** As you make your plans to become a successful entrepreneur, you need to have goals along the way to be achieved. These goals could be related to income, lifestyle, passion, or anything that might be important to you. The important thing is not

really what the goals are but that these goals are being achieved. If they are not, then why are you taking the risk and making all these sacrifices? At the end of the day, your business won't be evaluated on how hard you worked and how much of a risk you took but on whether you achieved your goals. If you did not, then it is highly unlikely that you will still be in business.

Entrepreneurship is not something to be feared. However, it is definitely something to be respected and researched before you begin. Start with understanding the risks that you will need to take, the sacrifices you will need to make, and the goals you will need to achieve. This may not guarantee you success, but it will definitely position you for it.

Session Review Questions: What are some things that you are willing to sacrifice for the success of your business and what things are you not?

COACHING SESSION 6

Questions to Answer before Moving from Full-Time Employee to Full-Time Business Owner

> Great achievement is usually
> born of great sacrifice, and is
> never the result of selfishness.
> —NAPOLEON HILL, AUTHOR OF
> *THINK AND GROW RICH*

As I speak to individuals who are contemplating making the move from full-time employment to becoming full-time business owners, there is always a ton of enthusiasm and energy behind their vision. And for that, I commend each and every one of them, as that is exactly what they will need in order to become successful as entrepreneurs. Sometimes though, I also have to temper that enthusiasm by making sure they understand some of the differences in expectations by asking the following questions.

1. **How do you feel about fluctuating income?** As an employee, you may not get paid as much as the owner of the business but more than likely, you receive a steady income at the end of every pay period. Once you move to the world of business ownership, the ability to depend on a steady income becomes much less reliable. We hope your income will increase from month to month, but it is almost a certainty that the income will fluctuate as you learn the best way to run your business.

2. **Are you okay with being paid last?** As an employee, you get paid first. Your expectation is that, regardless of how the business does, you will still get paid. When you own the business, there is a chance that some weeks, you may not get paid at all even though the business does well. In order for you to get paid as the business owner, not only does the business have to do well but you have to manage the expenses properly. Most business owners realize real soon that, most of the time, they will get paid after the employees, the utility company, the landlord, the bank, and so on.

3. **How much are you willing to invest in yourself?** The first thing most employees look for when they join a company is the benefits package. They want to know how much the company is willing to invest in them. When you own the business, you have to determine early on what you are willing to invest in it. This is actually the same thing as "investing in yourself." The majority of the

time, the money to start your small business will not come from a bank or an angel investor. It will come from your savings account, stock options, or retirement plan.

4. **Is this business all about the money?** The main reason employees look for a job is for income. They want to put in a certain amount of time for a certain amount of pay, which is definitely fair. In order to become a successful business owner, your motivation needs to be more than just the desire to make money. The amount of time, effort, and energy that you will have to put into the business will require more than a monetary outcome, in most cases. Entrepreneurs appreciate the control that owning a business affords them. And this control can be exhibited in many ways. For example, choosing the hours of operation, hiring only people you would like to work with, selling products and services "your way," and more. These perks provide that extra motivation to make the business work when the money coming in is not enough.

Even though these questions are simple and straightforward, many times, they spark the additional consideration that my clients need to make sure that the change from employee to business owner is truly the right one for them.

Session Review Question: How will investing in a business affect your personal lifestyle?

COACHING SESSION 7

People Entrepreneurs Need on Their Teams

> The fastest way to change yourself
> is to hang out with people who are
> already the way you want to be.
> —REID HOFFMAN, COFOUNDER OF LINKEDIN

During my initial coaching sessions with new clients, I frequently notice a common problem. Most of them want to do everything themselves. And though initially, they may be able to do it, there will come a time when they will have to get help, especially if they want to grow their businesses and maintain mental stability. Since I am not a licensed psychiatrist and won't be able to provide medical support, I try to help them avoid potential mental instability by recommending that they have the following five people identified for their support teams.

1. **Assistant**—There will be so many tasks required when you start your business that an assistant will be a must. As an entrepreneur, you have to stay focused on executing the strategic vision and not get bogged down in working on every single task. Sometimes, what is even worse is that some tasks are missed altogether because they get overlooked. An assistant can help make sure that these important small things are done.

2. **Attorney**—The legal structure of your new business is one of the most important decisions you can make. Most budding entrepreneurs have no idea if a sole-proprietor, partnership, corporation, or LLC structure will be the best match for them. Legal expertise on the front end can help you get that decision right from the onset and avoid unnecessary expenses on the back end. Attorneys can also review legal documents and provide insight before you enter into any contracts.

3. **Accountant**—If your business does not make money, it probably does not make any sense. That's why having a person to watch the income and make recommendations on the best way to track and manage your money is crucial. And what might be the most important thing is that they can handle reporting your taxes to the IRS and any audits that might occur.

4. **Mentor**—Having a mentor is crucial to an entrepreneur's success. A mentor can accelerate your learning curve by providing perspective. The

mentor's experience will help you avoid any of his or her mistakes or reduce the amount of time spent spinning your wheels in situations that he or she is familiar with. A mentor entrepreneur can also help you by providing access to his or her own network, which in most cases will be more mature and resourceful than yours.

5. **Coach**—With so many ideas in your mind and that same number of tasks or more on your to-do list, you'll find that a coach will play a crucial part in your success. Your coach will act as your thought partner by helping you prioritize responsibilities, assisting you to define your execution strategy, and then following up to hold you accountable for the execution. He or she will help take you from "I want to" to "I will."

As an entrepreneur, you will not be able to be an expert in everything; therefore, you have to surround yourself with other people to help fill in those gaps. Your team will be critical to your success, so get the right people on board to provide expert advice and to keep you on track to what is important in building a strong, sustainable business model.

Session Review Questions: Besides you, who will be the most important person on your team and why?

COACHING SESSION 8

Signs that You Need to Own Your Own Business

> Your time is limited, so don't waste
> it living someone else's life.
> —STEVE JOBS, COFOUNDER OF APPLE

As I take on new clients, I always have conversations with them to determine how they know that entrepreneurship is the right path for them and when they knew it was time for them to start their own businesses. Since I have asked these questions over one thousand times, I have started to notice some trends that may benefit you as you try to make the same decision. Here are the top three times I have identified as when the idea to become "your own boss" takes hold:

1. **No damn raise**—There is no more powerful reflection point in one's career than when your boss tells you that you had a solid year

performance-wise, but due to budget consider-ations, your employer is not giving out raises this year or only increasing your salary 1 to 3 percent. Even though this might be a raise, it sometimes barely keeps up with inflation. Data from the US Inflation Calculator shows the inflation rate has averaged about 2.3 percent over the last ten years.[2] So if you are the lucky one who gets the 3 percent raise, you will have an additional 0.7 per-cent in buying power each year. Over time, that becomes a hard pill to swallow, and my clients decide that they want to create their own raises.

2. **Need a new lifestyle**—It might surprise some, but a similar number of my clients have made the "become your own boss" decision based on improving their lifestyle as those who were tired of not getting raises. Many people well into their careers become tired of their daily commute, working long hours, consistent business travel, and perpetual layoffs. These factors and oth-ers contribute to missing milestone moments with family, poor health conditions, and daily dread. Even though they are aware that starting a business might reduce their income, they have realized that, to them, money is not the most important thing.

3. **I'm better than my boss**—Is it hard to believe that some people are smarter and more efficient than

2 US Inflation Calculator, accessed July, 10 2016, http://www.usinflationcalculator.com/inflation/current-inflation-rates/.

their bosses? Well, most of my clients claim that they are, and since I do not know their bosses, I am not in any position to argue with them. We have all heard stories about people being over-looked for promotions or reaching that glass ceiling because of limited opportunities. And I think we all have either had a challenging boss or had a friend or family member who has, so it is safe to say it is a common experience. In these cases, there are really only two choices: change jobs and hope you get a better boss or create your own business and really show your boss that you are smarter than he or she is. My clients choose the latter and use this situation to fuel their entrepreneurial fire.

Sometimes, there will be more than just one sign that will provide that last push necessary for a person to take that big step into the world of entrepreneurship. Regardless of the reason why it happens, the key is to recognize that entrepreneurship is your next step and prepare accordingly.

Session Review Question: What was the moment that made you aware that entrepreneurship was for you?

COACHING SESSION 9

Prepare Your Family for the World of Entrepreneurship

> Tough times never last; tough
> people always do.
> —ROBERT HERJAVEC, FOUNDER OF THE
> HARJAVEC GROUP AND MEMBER OF *SHARK TANK*

When an entrepreneur begins his or her first business or launches a new one, there is always concern for his or her own well-being and that of the business, but it is rare that I see that same concern for those who will be impacted as significantly by this move—the family. Venturing into the world of entrepreneurship will be a life-changing experience. This change will be either for the good or for the bad. Some statistics show that only about 40 percent of new businesses are successful after the five-year mark, so unfortunately, opening a new business has a great chance of the change being difficult. Knowing that the family's life is going to change as well, it is only fair (and smart) that any entrepreneur brings them into the loop by taking the following steps:

1. **Discuss the why.** When an entrepreneur starts to consider opening a business, he or she should tell the family why. Why is the path of entrepreneurship being taken? Is it because there is a need to provide more money, a better lifestyle, or more time with the family? Sharing this up front helps everyone know why the family's lifestyle and interactions will change, so that the entrepreneur already has buy-in from his or her most important support system during some of the challenging times they will all face.

2. **Start making adjustments immediately.** Due to the need to invest in the business financially, it will be in the best interest of the family for everyone to know that there may be a change to their lifestyle. For instance, it could be as big as canceling the annual summer vacation every year, as some of that money will need to be used for the new business, or as small as not going out to eat every weekend as a family for that same reason.

3. **Report out.** Make sure the family is aware of how the business is progressing. Everyone needs to be aware of how the new business is trending. If it is going well, then this update can provide those who have a natural tendency to worry the reassurance they need to sleep well at night. And at those times where there may be a need to tighten

the belt more, a report out can help reduce the resentment that some might have toward this new business infringing on their lifestyle and time with you.

4. **Be honest.** The old saying that "honesty is the best policy" definitely holds true for those family discussions. It is a must to lead with the positive potential outcomes that can be expected to come from launching a new business, but there also has to be a common understanding, on the other end, of the potential pitfalls that could take place. When times become challenging or take an unanticipated turn, a business owner needs to make sure that no one who depends on him or her feels misled.

Know that there are no guarantees in life and that a significant number of entrepreneurs launch two or three businesses before achieving a level of success; it is only fair that the most informed people should be the entrepreneur's family. If not, there is the unfortunate potential that the entrepreneur could also be on a second or third family before obtaining the level of success he or she aspires to.

Session Review Question: How will the people that depend on you for support be impacted by your decision to start a business?

COACHING SESSION 10

Signs that You Own a Job, Not a Business

> Simply put, your job is to prepare
> yourself and your business for growth.
> —MICHAEL E. GERBER, AUTHOR
> OF *THE E-MYTH REVISITED*

I often have the opportunity to work with great people who have already found the path to entrepreneurship and have successfully been in business for years. Our conversations, therefore, are not centered around what type of businesses they should start and how to go about it. These conversations are more about finding ways for them to take their businesses to the next level, as many feel as though they have plateaued. In order for me to help these clients, I first have to ask the following questions to make sure that I am talking to someone who owns a business and not a job.

1. **Do you make money when you are away?** This question is pretty straightforward, as it provides

insight and is the foundation to many other follow-up questions. If the response to this question
is, "No," then you own a job. The reason being is
that if you are not producing income while you
are sleeping, on vacation, or may be home ill,
then you are only being paid when you actually
work. Simply put as a business owner, you make
money when other people work.

2. **Do you handle everything?** Let's say that you got
stranded on a deserted island (which I know is
highly unlikely, but work with me here). Would
anybody else know how to run your business? For
example, would someone be able to pay the bills
or contact your client base if necessary? When
you own a business, one of the key components
is that you have administrative processes in place
to run in the absence of the owner. In *The E-Myth*,
Michael Gerber stresses that most small businesses plateau at some point because the owner
tries to do everything him- or herself and does
not create processes that can be duplicated.

3. **Does everyone know that you own a business?** A
key component to growing and sustaining any
business is consistent marketing. A good sign
that you are running a business is if everyone
you know is aware that you actually own a business. If they do not know what goods and services you provide, how do they know to come
to you when they actually need one of your
services? I encourage aspiring entrepreneurs
to look at marketing as an investment in the

business rather than an expense, which is what it is if you only own a job.

4. **Can you sell it for a profit?** Out of all the questions that I ask to determine if entrepreneurs actually own a business, this is the toughest one for people to swallow. The reason, I have come to find, is that the majority of the time, the answer is a resounding, "No." The cause of this response is that when most people start a small business, they only look at it as a job—a way to create an income for a fixed time and not something that can eventually be sold for a profit. When you start out with the mentality that you may eventually want to sell, how you structure and create processes for your business is important. And it will be even more important to whoever would want to buy it.

It is safe to say that owning a job is easier than running a business, so I do understand when entrepreneurs go in that direction. But another question I ask is: If a job is all you want, isn't it just easier to get a job in the first place? It takes clients some time to answer this question, if they even do at all.

Session Review Question: What have you done so far to make sure you will not (or do not currently) own a job?

COACHING SESSION 11

Why a Business Plan Is an Entrepreneur's Best Friend

> Formal education will make you a living;
> self-education will make you a fortune.
> —JIM ROHN, ENTREPRENEUR,
> MOTIVATIONAL SPEAKER, AND AUTHOR
> OF *THE ART OF EXCEPTIONAL LIVING*

It takes a strong person to start a business and keep it running. As time goes on, the obstacles that you face and overcome will make you a better, more mature entrepreneur. Research by the Kauffman Foundation of Entrepreneurship relates that 40 percent of businesses fail after two years, but for an aspiring entrepreneur, the potential success outweighs the potential of failure. This can be one of the biggest risks you take in life, but if planned correctly, it will be the most rewarding. Speaking of plan…did you know that a basic business plan can be an entrepreneur's best friend?

There is a significant amount of debate regarding the value of a business plan, from how long it should be to how often it should be updated. The most telling statistic that I have heard is that 80 percent of businesses that fail never had a business plan. Now, you can take this statistic either of two ways. One, there are still 20 percent of businesses that make it without a business plan, or two, a majority of entrepreneurs who fail have no business plan at all. My years of experience coaching entrepreneurs makes me a fan of number two. Even though the detail of the business plan varies case by case, I encourage all entrepreneurs to complete some level of research prior to opening their businesses. I encourage them to consider a business plan as a new best friend, because it will provide the following:

1. **It will tell it like it is!** One the good things about some best friends is that they will tell you the truth when you need to hear it. A business plan will do the same thing if used properly. For instance, when you create a business plan, you will normally have projections on how much money you will need to spend and how much money you will earn. If you review your business plan regularly, each time you do, it will tell it like it is! If you are not meeting your goals, it will be pretty apparent. And depending on the detail of your plan, it will even tell you why you are not.

2. **It will go to battle for you.** Another trait of a best friend is that he or she will step up for you when you need it. Again, a business plan does this as well. Many entrepreneurs will eventually have

to reach out to others to acquire more capital to start or expand their businesses and, as many already know, acquiring money from banks or investors can be like going to war. A good business plan will go to battle with you and help show those investors that you mean business because you have a plan which convinces them that you have an idea which can actually make money and you know how to execute on that idea.

3. **It knows all your business.** Your best friend tends to have much more insight than anyone else into what's going on with and around you. He or she is the one person you feel comfortable telling everything to, and therefore, he or she knows all your business, including the good, the bad, and the ugly. A good business plan provides the same type of support. It will know everything about your business, from who your target customers are and how you make money to what your competitive advantages might be. The ugly part kicks in when you have a business that has none of these.

All of us need friends to support us in our endeavors. Entrepreneurs need even more support, based on the ups and downs that starting a business creates. If your business plan becomes one of your best friends, you increase the support around you and the chances that your business will be successful.

Session Review Question: Which one of your friends exhibits the traits you would most want in your business plan?

COACHING SESSION 12

Learn on Someone Else's Time

> If you think education is
> expensive, try ignorance.
> —DEREK BOK, PRESIDENT OF
> HARVARD UNIVERSITY

There are a lot of lessons that an entrepreneur will need to learn as he or she builds a business. Some of these lessons can be very expensive from a monetary standpoint, but what can be even more expensive is the amount of time that is lost making mistakes. Just for clarity, I am not suggesting that being able to avoid making any mistakes is possible, but there are a few ways that an entrepreneur can reduce the learning curve and increase their chances for success on somebody else's time. Consider the following before you launch your next great business idea.

1. **Create your own internship.** There is research which shows that the average entrepreneur

works six years for someone else before striking out on his or her own. And a significant number of these individuals spent time working in similar fields as their businesses. I consider this time to be equivalent to a paid internship, where they have had the opportunity to learn how to run a business. It is not even necessary that the internship be with the best business, because you will learn either way. You will want to duplicate the good things and avoid the bad things. For instance, let's say there is a great marketing plan that the business runs during your "paid internship" that it took three times to get right. You get to see the end result and how it works and the best way to run it the first time. This will save you money on the front end, by not having to experiment as much, and make you money faster on the back end because you will attract clients earlier.

2. **Find a mentor.** Having a mentor or mentors who have been entrepreneurs and owned their own businesses can be invaluable. The right mentor has already experienced many of the things that you will come across during your journey to success, and when there is a need to make a tough decision, you will have someone you can call for advice that you can trust. Your mentor can also help increase the pace of your business learning in another important way. Many times, he or she will already have an established business network that has been built up over the years that he or

she can tap into. Maybe you are having a challenge getting meetings with people to have your product placed, and your mentor has done business with those people in the past. It may be as simple as the mentor making a phone call for you to make that meeting happen.

3. **Become a student.** There is some debate whether a business degree is necessary to be a successful business owner. I am a big proponent of education, so if you have the opportunity to further your collegiate education, I definitely encourage it. But I also know that "going back to school" might not be the best business decision for some. So the question is: How do you learn on someone else's time? It is actually pretty simple; there are thousands of business books from successful entrepreneurs that you can choose to read or listen to on audio. Another great tool to help you learn from other business owners' experiences is listening to them on podcasts or watching videos. The great thing about these options is that there is a wide range of information to choose from with little expense, if any at all. Choose from classes on marketing your products or leading your team, or maybe you want industry-specific advice, ranging from the technology start-ups to starting a home-based business. There are a significant number of resources available.

Learning on someone else's time might sound like a selfish idea initially, but as entrepreneurs realize it is more about sharing in others' experiences, it becomes a more comfortable philosophy. By learning while you work in your current position, asking for advice from mentors, and taking the time to be a student of your business, you will do something that all entrepreneurs need to do: create the highest return possible on your initial investment. In this case, it will be a high return on the most valuable resource you have: your time!

Session Review Question: What do you need to learn at no cost that will help you increase the ROI in your business?

COACHING SESSION 13

What Type of Entrepreneur Are You?

> Entrepreneurship is neither a
> science nor an art. It is a practice.
> —PETER DRUCKER, AUTHOR OF
> *INNOVATION AND ENTREPRENEURSHIP*

After so many hours of coaching entrepreneurs, I have noticed that all entrepreneurs are not the same. This may be an obvious statement, since people are not the same, but even though entrepreneurs are not, they are similar in some ways. And one of the ways they are similar is related to the type of entrepreneur that they are. Even though you can find several classifications of entrepreneurs and people may move from one category to the other throughout their lifetime, there is value in identifying if you are one of the following types of entrepreneurs.

- **Serial entrepreneur**—This type of entrepreneur loves the thrill and challenge of starting a new business. These entrepreneurs enjoy taking an idea and making it become a reality. Whether it takes one, three, or five years, they are all in until the business is a success. Once the "thrill is gone," they are ready to sell the business and start over again or look to find another business to add to their portfolios. These entrepreneurs are always looking for the next great idea and are not afraid to take risks of all kinds.

- **Lifestyle entrepreneur**—This may be a surprise for some entrepreneurs, but not everyone who starts a business is focused on making a whole lot of money. Many actually want to create a way to live a certain type of lifestyle and create streams of income to align with that lifestyle. This may be the stay-at-home mom who starts a home-based business to create more income for the kids' after-school activities or the person who loves to work out and decides to become a personal trainer so he or she can stay in shape and make money at the same time. Either way, on their path to entrepreneurship, the ability to live a certain way is as important as the income the business provides.

- **Sidepreneur**—You may be surprised there is a name for an entrepreneur who actually has a full-time job and choses to work on the side. Some people may know this by the name of "hustler" rather than sidepreneur, but they are one and the same. Individuals who choose to run a business on the side are typically motivated by creating additional income as a supplement to what they are currently making. I also have worked with several who use it as a bridge from full-time employment to being a full-time business owner. They begin working their side businesses so that they can make a smooth transition when the big day comes and they decide—or in some cases have to—go out on their own.

- **Social entrepreneur**—People who fall into this category tend to create businesses whose main focus is to help others. Their primary drive is to solve a social ill or improve the quality of life for those they choose to help. These entrepreneurs are philanthropists, social activists, environmentalists, and other social-oriented practitioners who use business philosophies in their work. For these entrepreneurs, money is not the driving factor. The ability to effect change by applying business theories and processes is the outcome they desire. One of the most impactful social entrepreneurship ideas for entrepreneurs has been the creation of microloan companies. These are companies that focus on providing loans to small businesses that would not traditionally qualify for one because of no established credit or the loan being too small. This business model has impacted millions across the world, especially in underdeveloped countries, where a hundred-dollar loan allows you start a business that helps you to feed your family.

The entrepreneurial path can lead you in many directions, so it is important to know from the onset which direction to take. By taking the right path, you won't get lost on the journey to opening several businesses or changing the world by starting just one.

Session Review Question: Which type of entrepreneur are you most like?

COACHING SESSION 14

Some Illusions of Entrepreneurship

> Timing, perseverance, and ten years
> of trying will eventually make you
> look like an overnight success.
> —BIZ STONE, COFOUNDER OF TWITTER

I have noticed that many entrepreneurs come to me with an overwhelming sense of confidence that their idea to start a business is the best thing ever and there is no way they can fail. They have a million-dollar idea that they are confident can get to market and fantasize about how "cool" it will be to be an entrepreneur and pass out cards that say "owner" or "CEO." Don't get me wrong; it *is* cool, but as "The Reality Coach" for entrepreneurs, one of my primary duties is to clear up the following illusions for my clients.

- **Anybody can do it!** I had the experience of working with clients who came to me after they had visited a local community where they saw a booming business area with streets lined with thriving small businesses. After seeing all of that success, they came to me, saying that they were inspired to get the ball rolling with their own business because if all these people could do it, why couldn't they? The fact is about seven out of ten new businesses will close within the first ten years. And over 50 percent of those closings will take place during the first three. Many times, entrepreneurs only see the successful businesses that actually made it, not the two or three others that failed in that same location first.

- **It can't be that hard. All the entrepreneurs I know are doing well.** Most of the entrepreneurs that I have worked with state over and over that starting and running a business was the hardest thing that they have ever done in their careers, so it surprises some future business owners when I tell them this. Most people see successful entrepreneurs once they have made it, not during the times of struggle and sacrifice that took place when the business actually first opened. Also, as most people do in their personal lives, business owners put on a good face for their employees and customers even when things are going extremely badly behind the scenes. Even if you ask them how they are doing, they will say things are going well. I think we all have had the experience of seeing a business that we frequented close to our surprise, because we thought they were actually doing so well.

- **Most people get it right on their first try.** Another illusion is that most entrepreneurs get it right the first time out. Some surveys show that less than 10 percent of entrepreneurs are successful when they start their first businesses. People may argue the percentage, but it is a fact that you are more likely to fail your first time out. One of the characteristics that stands out for success as an entrepreneur is tenacity. Many times, entrepreneurs who are deemed as overnight successes are actually not; they have failed one or more times, and the lessons they learned from past mistakes have increased their chances for success.

Some may feel that shining light on these illusions will convince many people not to become entrepreneurs. I actually agree with this statement. And I would hope it does! Not everyone is meant to be an entrepreneur, and if a simple coaching conversation deters someone from opening a business, my opinion is that this person doesn't have the confidence or resilience needed to be an entrepreneur in the first place. There is something for people who aren't wired to be entrepreneurs. It is called a job.

Session Review Question: Which one of these illusions have you had to deal with?

Entrepreneur's Reality Check:
"Recognize obstacles, but don't
be intimidated by them.
You need to WIN, no matter
what!"

- Roddric W. Sims
www.SimsCoachingGroup.com

Section One Takeaways: Exposure

What quote will you share?

_____
_____
_____

Whom will you share it with?

_____

Which coaching session resonated with you the most?
And why?

_____
_____
_____
_____
_____

What was your biggest takeaway from this section?

_____
_____
_____

What three actions are you ready to take now based on
what you've learned? And by when?

    1. _____ Date: _____
    2. _____ Date: _____
    3. _____ Date: _____

Who will be your accountability partner?

_____

What does success look like when you have accomplished your goals?

_____

_____

_____

_____

_____

What will you do to celebrate when these goals have been accomplished?

_____

_____

_____

Section Two

The 2nd E of Entrepreneurship—Economics

Economics[3]

- a science concerned with the process or system by which goods and services are produced, sold, and bought
- the part of something that relates to money

---

3 *Merriam-Webster*, s.v. "Economics," accessed July 10, 2016, http://www.merriam-webster.com/dictionary/economics.

COACHING SESSION 15

The Cost of Entrepreneurship

> I'd say it's been my biggest problem
> all my life…it's money. It takes a lot of
> money to make these dreams come true.
> —WALT DISNEY, COFOUNDER OF
> THE WALT DISNEY COMPANY

When starting a new business, the biggest worries and roadblocks for most are the cost of getting the business up and running and where that money will actually come from. This is something that obviously has to be considered by any aspiring entrepreneur, but there are also some additional costs that should be examined even before those are determined. Many people don't see them, so let's make sure that you do before you jump into the deep end of the entrepreneurship pool.

1. **Income from old job**—When many decide to take on the world of entrepreneurship, they also choose to leave their old jobs behind. And with that, they leave their old income behind too. For those who have planned in advance for this change, this loss of income may be not be that significant, but for those who launch a business on a whim, the fact they do not have any income coming in is a significant adjustment. Even if the business does generate enough money to cover the old salary, there still is the adjustment to the way that the income is paid out. A job typically provides income every two weeks, and many depend on that consistency in their lives. The reality is that, as a new business owner, more than likely, your income will fluctuate from month to month and year to year. Hopefully, it will increase consistently, but there are no guarantees.

2. **Interest from savings**—Many times, the money used to start a small business comes from the personal savings of the entrepreneur. This savings may be from retirement plans, stocks and bonds, or a line of credit. Regardless of where the money comes from, there will be a loss of the opportunity to earn interest on any of the invested money. We hope that money and more will be returned to the source to cover the interest lost, but that is a risk which has to be taken.

3. **Career development**—Some research shows that the average business owner works at least seven years before going out on his or her own. During

this time of career development, there are a lot of opportunities for the business owner to gain special skills and receive raises and promotions. When the decision is made to leave, all that progress is left behind. And as he or she is building the new business, the same loss takes place. No promotions or raises will happen. Old coworkers will develop in their careers while the entrepreneur is building a business. Now, this may not be a big deal for those who go on to have or surpass the income expectations, but in those situations where the business does not develop and there is a need to return to the old career, the time loss can never be made up. Actually, some have to return to roles at lower levels than when they left—if in fact they can even return at all.

This list should in no way discourage the committed entrepreneur from running full steam to business ownership because these are all risks that have to be taken to be successful. Understanding these costs might not make the leap into the pool of entrepreneurship any different, but I am sure you agree it is easier to dive into a pool with your eyes wide open versus being blindfolded.

Session Review Question: What opportunities are you willing to sacrifice in order to become a successful entrepreneur?

COACHING SESSION 16

How Much Money Will You Really Need?

> If you don't educate yourself,
> you'll never get out of the starting
> block because you'll spend all your
> money making foolish decisions.
> —DAYMOND JOHN, FOUNDER OF FUBU
> AND MEMBER OF *SHARK TANK*

One of the great things about coaching entrepreneurs for a decade is that I have had the chance to ask a lot of established business owners questions that help me coach aspiring entrepreneurs. A favorite question of mine to ask is, "Knowing what you know now, what would you do differently?" With the types of businesses and products varying so much, I at first expected the responses to be all over the place. Now, I know better! I now expect to hear one common response the majority of the time. And that response is, "I would have had more money!" When I ask what the money would be used for is when the responses start to vary greatly.

One of the responses I hear the most is that the additional money would be used for start-up capital. Getting off to a strong start is huge factor in the success of a business. Typically, the better the start, the faster the business will make money. The use of this additional start-up capital can be focused on advertising before the product or service is launched so that the business can have customers on day one versus day thirty-one. And what many also shared was that they made mistakes with how the money was spent. These mistakes included investing in advertising that never brought in customers, paying for the training of employees who eventually had to be fired, and buying food that spoiled before it could be sold. Basically, more money was needed to cover the mistakes they made before the business even started.

Another reason why I hear more money would have been nice is for operating expenses. Typically, you will hear from a business school's curriculum you should have access to three to six months of operating expenses in reserve for your business. The main reason is for unexpected situations that might impact the businesses income. For instance, let's say you have someone on your team who is responsible for the majority of your monthly sales; the person becomes ill, and his or her two-week absence impacts the sales for the whole month. If you have a new business, this could be a huge setback, as the business may be operating month to month and may be dependent on those sales to pay the rent. Having money in reserve will allow for the business to keep going until the sales catch back up over the next few months. The other benefit of having more money for operating expenses is that there may be other potential opportunities that come up in the business that you didn't expect, and having extra capital will let you take advantage of them and grow your business even faster.

Last but not least, there was a desire to have more money for personal expenses. The first question may be: What do personal expenses have to do with the business expenses? Well, in a best-case scenario, nothing. But in the real world, some clients have shared with me that money had to be pulled out of the business at times to manage their expenses at home. This tends to occur when people leave a job to open a business full-time. They go from making money to having to invest money in a business monthly, which, simply put, means they are operating at a deficit. So they have had to pull some of the money from the business to keep the lights on at home.

When I am asked by someone how much money he or she should have to open a business, my response is, "What is the most you can get?" At the end of the day, the goal should be to have access to as much investment capital as possible. The hope is that you will not need to use it all, but it is always better for you and your business to have more and not need it than to have only enough and use it all.

Session Review Question: How will your current income be impacted by starting a business?

COACHING SESSION 17

Investment Versus Expense: Make Sure You Know the Difference

> Never stop investing. Never
> stop improving. Never stop
> doing something new.
> —BOB PARSONS, FOUNDER OF GODADDY

As you start planning for your business, one of the most important things that you will need to know and manage will be the expenses. Most times, when I have this conversation with clients, they either appear to roll up into a ball and try to avoid the conversation or become combative, as if I have just cursed at them! Either situation can be tense for both of us, so to make it easier, I have started making sure that my clients know the difference between an investment and an expense.

When you start projecting all the related costs to opening a business, it can really become depressing as you look at all of the money going out, from basic utilities that all business have, like electricity, Internet, and telephone service, to costs related specifically to your business, like materials, equipment, and specialized services. There is always a cost to do business. How much that amount will be depends on the type of business. My clients who get through this process with smiles on their faces have realized that most of the costs are investments rather than just expenses. We get to this place by redefining any cost as an investment if it directly impacts the sales of the business. For example, in a coffee shop, the customer service skills of the barista and the quality of coffee determine if a customer will return. The salary of the barista and the price of the coffee are therefore investments because they yield a "return on the investment." In this example, the ROI happens to be returning customers, which leads to more sales. In other cases, it won't be as clear, and the ROI may be a calculation of combining a number of different aspects of your business together. Again, the easy way to determine if it is an investment is to see if it impacts your income.

Now that there is a clearer picture of what an investment is, we still have to discuss those expenses that do not impact the sales of your business. So, staying with our coffee shop model, let's say that every morning before the doors open, the owner brews a special cup of coffee that only he or she drinks and watches the morning news on the cable TV hookup in the office. Even though drinking coffee is what you do in a coffee shop and watching the news and drinking coffee go hand in hand, the cost of both would truly be expenses as neither one will directly impact the sales or the business. The coffee is a special blend only for the owner, and the cable TV is not for the customers either; it is a "perk" of ownership. (Sorry, I couldn't help but use that pun.) There is nothing wrong with either of these costs; they are just expenses that have no direct return on the sales of the business.

As a business owner, your goal is to make a profit, and that is accomplished by running a business efficiently. It is not only about sales, but also about managing the expenses. It is about having more income than expenses, and to go one step further, you will take home more money in the long run if you have more investments than expenses.

Session Review Question: Which expenses of your business can be turned into investments?

COACHING SESSION 18

The Big 3 Expenses, or Should I Say, "Investments"

It's not about money or connections. It's
the willingness to outwork and outlearn
everyone when it comes to your business.
—MARK CUBAN, SERIAL ENTREPRENEUR
AND MEMBER OF *SHARK TANK*

In planning to start a business, there are a number of
expenses that have to be considered before an opening can take place. Since this can be an overwhelming task, I tend to recommend to my clients that they
get started by focusing on just a few items. Over the
years, I have reviewed hundreds of business plans and
have come to notice that there are three areas that most
entrepreneurs anticipate where they will spend most of
their money. Knowing these areas in advance will go a
long way with determining how to best prepare for your
journey into entrepreneurship, as combined, they will

typically make up more than 50 percent of your total business expenses. Let's review them one by one:

1. **People**—In most businesses, the biggest cost is associated with the people who are needed to help run the day-to-day operations. Depending on the business model, this could range from simply answering the phone all the way to helping with product design. The cost of people is significantly tied up in payroll, which is considered their salary, commissions, and bonus structure. Also, there is a little thing called health benefits that needs to be provided for small businesses that have fifty or more employees which has to be considered as the business grows. And when you attach the possibility of providing vacation and holiday pay, as well as other ancillary benefits, the "people" cost becomes more and more substantial. We witness the impact that payroll costs have on the business world every day in the news when big companies who are struggling to meet their stock price for their investors announce another round of layoffs as a quick fix to impact the bottom line.

2. **Promotions**—Each business, especially a *new* business, has to be aware of the need to promote its brand through marketing and advertising. The more competitive the market, the more important it is to have a marketing budget that makes your business or brand stand out from everyone else's. In some situations, this can be

the biggest expense an entrepreneur may have. On the advertising side, these expenses are seen in the form of billboards, flyers, commercials, direct mail, internet advertisements, and so on. And on the marketing side, there are lead purchasing services, referral programs, and customer loyalty initiatives, to name a few.

3. **Place**—"Location! Location! Location!" is a famous statement that you may have heard before. It stresses that in some businesses, where you are located is one of the most important things for long-term success. The advent of technology has diminished some of the importance of this principle for certain industries, but regardless of the location, the expense to acquire and maintain it can be quite significant. Alongside the mortgage or rent to lease the space, there will be a need to have phone/Wi-Fi, cleaning services, furniture, cable television, computers, and so on. By themselves, these expenses may not seem like much, but when you actually start adding them up, the realization occurs that having a place of business can put you out of business if you don't identify and manage all the costs related to having an actual location.

Entrepreneurs can't be scared of the expenses of starting and running a new business. The only way to truly develop a model that works is by investing in the business to determine the most efficient way for it to run. If the people, promotions, and places are considered more investments than expenses, then the focus will become more on the return on each investment rather than just the amount spent. And once you are able to track the ROI on more than 50 percent of your expenses, then you are well on your way to having a successful and efficient business.

Session Review Questions: What is or will be the biggest investment that you will have in your business? What percentage of your overall expenses will it be?

COACHING SESSION 19

If It Doesn't Make Money, It Doesn't Make Cents!

> Most people fail to realize that in life,
> it's not how much money you make,
> it's how much money you keep.
> —ROBERT T. KIYOSAKI, AUTHOR
> OF *RICH DAD, POOR DAD*

As any entrepreneur starts to contemplate going into business for him- or herself, there are so many terms and concepts that would be beneficial to learn that he or she could spend the next couple of years in college classes, workshops, symposiums, and numerous other educational endeavors to prepare. The interesting thing is that one can complete all this, and there will still be surprises that will lead to additional lessons. Knowing that this will happen reinforces the fact that adaptability is crucial for any entrepreneur's success, and also knowing some of these key concepts in advance is just as crucial to getting off to a strong start.

The most common reason that entrepreneurs give for business failure is lack of *cash flow* or what some would also call *operating capital*. Most businesses don't make money as soon as the doors open. There is typically a growth process where the business has to pick up momentum and build a loyal customer base. None of this takes place overnight. In order for the business to stay open, there has to be enough capital available to operate the business until then. It does not matter how nice the product may be or how great the service is; if you cannot keep the doors open until enough cash flow is created, then failure is certain. How much cash flow is needed is calculated simply by adding up all your monthly expenses. Once this is completed, the logical next step will be to subtract this from your total monthly income to determine if you have a positive or negative cash flow. At the beginning, a negative cash flow is all right and, in many cases, actually expected. The important thing is that eventually your cash flow turns positive and stays that way.

Another term that every entrepreneur should become familiar with is *break even*. This refers to the time when the amount of money that is invested in the business equals the amount of money that it earns. I have to admit that many people are naïve and think that just because they are making money, the business is in good shape. The real proof that the business is going in the right direction is when you can pay back the start-up capital that you used to begin your business. A simple way to do this is to determine your start-up expenses in advance and then project how many months it will take to earn enough to cover those expenses. If your business will take $12,000 to start and you project your gross income will allow you to pay back $1,000/month, then your break-even point would be one year (twelve months). Make no mistake: until that time, your business is not profitable. Once you make your break-even point, you can then pay back everyone who invested in you, especially yourself. And many times, people will not even invest in you unless you can tell them when they will receive a return on their investment.

The term I spend most of my time going over with clients is *return on investment* (ROI). This term is important to know, as it provides entrepreneurs one of the best ways to help them make decisions on where to invest their money. Once you obtain your investment capital, there will many opportunities to spend your money, and there has to be a way to determine the best options to do that. This is where ROI is important. To make it simple, let's use $1 as the benchmark. If you spend $1 to create a product and you are able to charge $1.50 for it, then your ROI is 50 percent, which is a pretty good return but not always realistic. The goal when looking at ROI is to determine what will bring the highest return on each dollar spent. So if you could build the same product but at a higher quality for $1.10, you would either have to charge more or be comfortable with making less. In some cases, this might be a wise business decision, as the cheapest way is not always the best way, and people will pay more for higher quality and return to your business more often. If you don't understand this basic concept, you may always invest your capital in things that return you the least amount of money, and that is never the best business decision.

It would be great for every entrepreneur to go to business school, but for varying reasons, that is not possible. What is possible, though, is that every entrepreneur should understand basic concepts to determine when he or she is actually making money. If not, the entrepreneur will evaluate the success of his or her company on the direct feedback of customers regarding the quality of the business's services and products, which could be great. Unfortunately, providing the best services and products doesn't always make you profitable. Understanding your cash flow needs, how to get the best return on your investment, and when the business will break even does.

Session Review Question: How do you know that your business will make a profit?

COACHING SESSION 20

Entrepreneurs Need to Be Prepared to Show Themselves the Money!

> A savvy entrepreneur will not always
> look for investment money first.
> —DAYMOND JOHN, FOUNDER OF FUBU
> AND MEMBER OF *SHARK TANK*

There is a famous scene in the movie *Jerry Maguire* where the football star played by Cuba Gooding Jr. gets the main character played by Tom Cruise to yell, "Show me the *money!*" in order to get pumped up for his current contract negotiations. I know many entrepreneurs who wish it were just as easy for them to walk into a bank with a solid business plan and tell the banker to "Show me the *money!*" and walk out with all the investment capital they need. Unfortunately, this rarely is the case for first-time entrepreneurs or small business owners. The reality, in most cases, is that entrepreneurs have to show themselves the *money!*

The popularity of the dot-com era and the current popularity of tech start-ups have made the term *angel investor* a common one that aspiring business owners have dreams about. Since the majority of small business aren't associated with either industry, many people are shocked when they are unable to find those investors when they are ready to launch their own businesses. If you watch the popular show *Shark Tank*, where entrepreneurs come on to pitch their ideas, you should notice that the contestants already have a finished product that they have built, tested, and sold before they even appear on the show. This means that a significant amount of money and time has to be invested before you can even look for an angel.

Banks are another common option that come to mind for entrepreneurs, but only about 10 percent of those who apply for bank loans will actually receive a loan. This is because banks only make loans when they can guarantee a return on the investment, and a new business or entrepreneur without a track record of success has no guarantee of any return at all. Banks will also consider a loan if you have collateral to secure it, but most times, the loan is needed to acquire collateral to make the product or provide the service in the first place.

With no angel investor and no interest from the bank, entrepreneurs have to honestly show themselves the money, also known as "using their own money." Where does this money come from? It typically comes from the following three sources:

1. **Personal savings—** Most personal financial advisors encourage their clients to have three to six

months' of expenses in a checking or savings account in case there is an emergency. Some of those advisors might not classify investing in a business as an emergency, but if you have an opportunity that will increase your income or change your life for the better and don't have any other resources, then investing in your own business might just be that emergency.

2. **Retirement accounts**—Another option that many of my clients lean on is their retirement funds. Many people are averse to the risk of touching these funds, and the majority of the reasons are quite valid. Using your retirement cushion might be a tough pill to swallow, but if you consider investing in your retirement to be investing in yourself, wouldn't investing in your own business be the same thing?

3. **Lines of credit**—A very popular way that entre-preneurs obtain money to invest in their busi-nesses comes from obtaining lines of credit from various sources. One of the most popular has been the home equity loan line of credit. This is basically a second mortgage on your home that allows you to invest or pay off bills with higher interest rates. And don't forget those credit cards that mostly everyone has as well. Depending on the interest rate and payback requirements, this might be a very feasible option, especially if you qualify for low interest for six to twelve months or more.

As you begin to prepare yourself mentally to take the big step into entrepreneurship, you also have to prepare yourself financially. Before you can convince anyone else to invest in you, you will need to invest in yourself first. If you can't show yourself the money, do you really think someone else will?

Session Review Questions: How much and for how long are you willing to invest in a business and yourself?

COACHING SESSION 21

How Much Are You Willing to Invest in Yourself?

> Sweat equity is the most
> valuable equity there is.
> —MARK CUBAN, SERIAL ENTREPRENEUR
> AND MEMBER OF *SHARK TANK*

One of my most impactful questions to ask entrepreneurs is, "How much are you willing to invest in yourself?" I tend to receive varying responses to this question, but the three most common are the following:

1. "What do you mean?"
2. "As much as I need to!"
3. "I don't have a lot."

The great thing is that each response tells me something about where this future business owner's mind-set is in regard to the importance of investment capital.

My response to "What do you mean?" is something similar to this. Since, in a majority of cases, the money that is used by entrepreneurs to start small businesses will need to come from their own personal savings, loans, or lines of credit, the question is asking how much of your personal assets you are willing to invest in yourself. This is important to know for a few reasons. One of the most important things that has to be determined prior to opening a business is how much money will be needed to get the business open, which is called *start-up capital*, and then once that is done, how much will be needed to keep the "doors open" until enough money is made by the business to pay all of its monthly expenses, which is known as *operating capital*. If what you are willing and able to invest in yourself is less than the required start-up expense, then there is obviously a problem.

The ability and willingness to invest in your own business proves two things. The first is that you are actually in a financial position to be a business owner, and the second is that you are actually willing to "bet on yourself." This means a lot, because if and when you go to friends, family, and other potential investors, it will prove to them that you have actually been preparing and this business is not just a whim. It will also prove that you will have some skin in the game. Investors and lending institutions are more willing to invest in those who will have as much—or more—to lose as they do.

When I hear the second response—"As much as I need to!"—it typically means that this future business owner has not done his or her homework. If you have completed the necessary research about the start-up costs of your business, you should be able to estimate how much it will cost you to get the doors open and allow you to make sound business decisions on where you need to invest that money.

For instance, let's say that your research shows that it will cost $15,000 to start your business off the way you would like, and you only have access to $10,000. This does not mean that the business can't open; it may just mean it is time to make some tough business decisions. One might be the following: Do you really need to invest in that sign that is going to cost you $4,000? Maybe you can actually get by with the smaller one that costs you $2,000. In addition, that brand-new office furniture you had your eye on costs $5,000; it could also be bought from a reseller for $2,000. It may not be "brand new," but it will be brand new to that location, and no one will ever notice the few scratches from the previous owner. Making those decisions brings the costs down to $10,000, which means you can still plan for that grand opening. Determining how much start-up capital you will need in advance will allow you to spend your money more wisely. What if you had spent the $4,000 on the sign already and, because it is a custom job, it cannot be returned? Now, you might really be in a position where you don't have as much as you need.

The last response—"I don't have a lot"—is probably the one I hear the most, and I can definitely appreciate the honesty and openness associated with it. In these cases, it might not be about the business that you want to open but more about the business that you can afford to open. If your goal is to create a business that allows you to live a certain lifestyle or to create extra income, then does it really matter what the business is? If not, there are hundreds if not thousands of businesses that can be started for a very small investment. One of the major impacts of technology has been that the cost of opening a business has declined significantly, and conversely, the number of home-based businesses has increased. These microbusinesses can be started with as little as $3,000 in some cases.

If the type of business is important and it costs more to open than you have, then the options now are to wait until you are able to save more money or find that friend or family member who is willing to invest in you as much as you are willing to invest in yourself. For some coaches, *waiting* is a bad word, but in situations related to opening your own business, it can be the most important word that I ever provide to my clients. Surveys show that it is not the idea, location, business model, or service that causes most businesses to fail; in fact, it is not having enough cash flow to invest and grow the business. If waiting six months to a year increases your chance at success by allowing time to save or acquire more investment capital, then it is worth the wait.

When preparing to open a business, the willingness to invest in yourself is a must. If you are not willing to invest in the biggest asset, which is you, why would anyone else want to?

Session Review Question: How much money will it take to successfully launch your business?

COACHING SESSION 22

How to Start a Business for Free

> I am not a product of my circumstances.
> I am a product of my decisions.
> —STEPHEN COVEY, AUTHOR OF *THE 7*
> *HABITS OF HIGHLY SUCCESSFUL PEOPLE*

A lot of aspiring entrepreneurs face a similar challenge to getting started in their businesses. And that challenge is the expense related to start-up cost. In a perfect world, each person who wants to open a business would be able to go to a bank or call his or her rich uncle for a loan. Unfortunately, my experience reveals that the majority of my clients don't have access to either. If start-up costs are the only thing holding you back from jumping into the world of entrepreneurship, consider the following:

1. **Home-based business**—One of the most significant fixed expenses that a business can have is the

rent or mortgage for its office. Most of the time, you are signing a lease and committing to monthly payment for three to five years, regardless of how well your business is doing from month to month. With the advent of home computers, video conferencing, and cell phones, more and more people are deciding to avoid this expense and become "homepreneurs." There are an estimated 30 million households with active home offices every week.[4] The same research relates that seven out of ten of these businesses succeed, which is significant, as it is twice the ratio expected for new businesses. Even though there are several factors that go into a business's success, I am confident that not having to worry about how you are going to pay the lease for the office helps with your monthly cash flow.

2. **Bartering**—I am always surprised by the negative response that I get when I mention bartering to clients. Most people only consider it for an exchange of goods, but there are also several opportunities for aspiring entrepreneurs to barter for essential services. For example, a social media client of mine bartered with an attorney in order to have legal advice provided for her business and in exchange, she managed the attorney's

---

4 Kenneth Rapooza, "One in Five Americans Work From Home, Numbers Seen Rising Over 60%," *Forbes*, February, 18 2013, accessed July 10, 2016, http://www.forbes.com/sites/kenrapoza/2013/02/18/one-in-five-americans-work-from-home-numbers-seen-rising-over-60/#69170b754768.

social media campaign for a designated amount of time. Even though she did pay based on the time spent, this was not an out-of-pocket expense she had to incur. This will not be the answer in every case, but you might be surprised what people would be willing to barter for your services.

3. **Freelancing**—A *freelancer* or *freelance worker* is a term commonly used for a person who is self-employed and is not necessarily committed to a particular employer long-term. The beauty of being a freelancer is that you have little to no overhead to manage for your business. You are a one-person shop, so you do not have to worry about meeting payroll and a huge office space, if any at all. Other businesses and entrepreneurs need freelancers to come in to perform specific tasks for a certain amount of time. Freelancing allows you to turn a specific skill you already possess into a business without needing to invest in a permanent infrastructure to support it.

Going out on your own is tough enough, so when you have the desire to be your own boss but not the resources available to do so, it can be discouraging. Those who have the right entrepreneurial spirit can turn that discouragement into creativity and figure out a way to make it work on limited resources.

Session Review Question: What creative ways will you use to reduce your expenses?

Entrepreneur's Reality Check:
"Success always COSTS.
You just have to be willing to
PAY THE PRICE!"

- Roddric W. Sims
www.SimsCoachingGroup.com

Section Two Takeaways: Economics

What quote will you share?

_____
_____
_____

Whom will you share it with?

_____

Which coaching session resonated with you the most?
And why?

_____
_____
_____
_____
_____

What was your biggest takeaway from this section?

_____
_____
_____
_____

What three actions are you ready to take now based on
what you've learned? And by when?

1. _____ Date: _____
2. _____ Date: _____
3. _____ Date: _____

Who will be your accountability partner?

_____

What does success look like when you have accomplished your goals?

_____

_____

_____

_____

_____

What will you do to celebrate when these goals have been accomplished?

_____

_____

_____

Who will be your accountability partner?

Section Three

The 3rd E of Entrepreneurship— Environment

Environment[5]

- the conditions that surround someone or something
- the conditions and influences that affect the growth, health, progress, etc., of someone or something

---

5 *Merriam-Webster*, s.v. "Environment," accessed July 10, 2016, www.merriam-webster.com/dictionary/economics.

COACHING SESSION 23

Do You Have a Million-Dollar Idea?

> High expectations are the
> key to everything.
> —SAM WALTON, FOUNDER OF WALMART

As I meet with new clients for the first time, I ask them several questions to determine where they are in the stage of business development. One of the most thought provoking questions that I ask them is: Do you have a million-dollar idea? Some are quick to jump into their business model and talk about ROI and break-even points. These people, I am confident, have a million-dollar idea and tend to tell me how soon they will make a million dollars without even knowing it. Others tend to hesitate, fumble around with their words, or just flat out admit that they do not have any idea. The reason that this question is important to answer is because it will help the aspiring entrepreneur determine if the investment of time and energy to start the new business is worth it.

Before we go any further with this concept, let me define what I mean by a million-dollar idea (MDI). An MDI is an idea that will allow you to make a million dollars. It's pretty plain and simple, isn't it? There is not even a time limit or a number of products sold/services provided, but just: Will this idea make you at least $1 million? The reason I use this number is that, from my experience watching the amount of energy and sacrifice that successful entrepreneurs invest into their businesses, there has to be an equitable financial return. I have had aspiring entrepreneurs say that if they aren't profitable for years that it will be okay, as it is not only about the money. I actually have had the chance to monitor the success of some of these individuals three years or more out, and what I can say for sure is that those who had an MDI are happier than those who did not. After hearing some of the trials and tribulations it took to succeed, I sometimes question if this number is even high enough!

The ability to answer this question provides insight into how much research the person has done into his or her idea. And for me, this equates to how serious he or she is about turning the idea into reality. There is a statement that goes something like this: "If it doesn't make money, it doesn't make sense." I have taken the liberty of tweaking it for business owners. My version goes, "If you don't know how your business makes money, then you don't make sense!"

It is actually not that difficult to determine if you have an MDI. If your idea is a product and you plan to make a one-dollar profit on each one sold, then that means you will need to sell one million products. Now, depending on the product, that could be a big deal or it could just be a tip of the iceberg because you may expect to sell two or three million. On the other hand, if selling one million is a stretch and selling five hundred thousand is more realistic, that is okay—you still possibly have an MDI. If you can increase your profit margin by another dollar so that you can make a two-dollar profit on each sale, your numbers will still work out. So, no longer is the question can you make a million dollars, it becomes how long will it take?

Session Review Questions: So, do you have a million-dollar idea? How do you know?

COACHING SESSION 24

Does Anyone Really Want What You Have?

> You must be very patient, very
> persistent. The world isn't going
> to shower gold coins on you just
> because you have a good idea.
> —HERB KELLEHER, FOUNDER
> OF SOUTHWEST AIRLINES

One of my most memorable clients was actually one of my shortest-term clients. He had not just come up with a million-dollar idea, but based on his projections, he had a billion-dollar idea. Initially, I was excited and thought that he might become my client forever. He definitely would be able to afford me! As I started reviewing his business plan in more detail, though, I came to the realization that he had made a significant mistake in estimating the market for his business. His numbers revealed that everyone—and I mean everyone—in the area would want his service.

The expectations were so high that it made me question if there had actually been any real research into the demand for the product, which led to one simple question that ended our coaching relationship. That question was, "Does anyone really want what you have?"

You might think that the relationship ended because my client thought that my question was harsh or insensitive, but that is not why. The reason it ended was because of the following.

Once he got over the initial shock of the question, he realized that he actually did not know the answer to it. Because the idea had come to him like a "gift from above," he had just assumed that everyone would receive it with open arms. And even though I agreed with him that it was a good idea, he had not done any research to determine if there was a market for it. Just because there is a certain population of people in an area does not guarantee that they will do business with you. There is a need to research and identify your clients. Identifying your clients will allow you to reach out to them or at least complete research to determine if, how, and when they would want your product. This can be done many ways. Common examples are by creating simple surveys that can be completed online, putting together focus groups, or investing money into acquiring data from research firms. Once the appropriate research is complete, you should know the age, gender, income range, and even the spending habits of your future customers.

My follow-up question appeared to be even more concerning to him. It was: "Who is your competition?" With billions of people in the world, there are fewer and fewer unique ideas. This means there is a signifi-cant chance that someone may have had a similar idea and has either launched a business already or is in the process of doing so. In either case, before determin-ing how profitable his business would be, he needed to know what the competition charged for the product. If the identified clients are accustomed to paying five dollars for the product and you planned to sell it for ten dollars, then you might have to lower your price to meet the customer's established pricing expectations. This means you may have to sell at least twice as much to make the desired income.

A few days passed, and I received an e-mail from this client, saying that he would not be moving forward with his idea, as he had done some additional research and determined that several people had already had a simi-lar one and had been in business for a few years already. Even though he thought it was still a solid opportunity, he felt that the competition would be too steep and decided to wait on the next idea.

His research made it obvious that someone wanted the product, but it also revealed that he would need to convince people that his product was the best. So, even though there was a desire for the product, he still would need to convince them to buy from him, which led back to the original question: "Does anyone really want what you have?"

Session Review Question: What are the demographics of your target customer?

COACHING SESSION 25

Identify Your Competition

> Whatever you do, be different—that
> was the advice my mother gave me,
> and I can't think of better advice
> for an entrepreneur. If you're
> different, you will stand out.
> —Anita Roddick, founder
> of the Body Shop

I get calls on a regular basis from aspiring entrepreneurs with some great ideas. These ideas are what I classify as million-dollar ideas because of the significant amount of potential they have. They range from simple products to complex services that can be delivered worldwide. Having the potential to market a product or service to the world is a great opportunity, but since I am of a belief that there are no unique ideas, I also know that more than likely there is someone else already executing on that idea somewhere else in the world. I encourage any entrepreneur to identify and learn what he or she can from the competition to make the most of a million-dollar idea.

Identifying the competition can be a significant amount of work itself, but it is a must if you truly want to enter a very competitive and mature marketplace or are trying to carve out your own niche in a newer market that has the potential to take off. Identifying your competition will help you identify how aggressive you will need to be as you start out. For example, if you are opening a service business in a community and there are three other similar businesses in a ten-mile radius, then you may need to be very aggressive in your marketing before you even open your doors so that your target market knows there is a newer and (you hope) better option in town. If not, when you open your doors, the community will maintain its old habits and pass you up on the way to the competition.

Figuring out who your competition will be will also allow you to determine if they have a competitive advantage. The competitive advantage could be based on price, location, quality of service, and so on. Once you learn these things, you can also determine if you can compete with them and what your competitive advantage may be. Let's say that after you research the other three businesses that you found in the community, you determine that they all have the same business hours during the week and are not open on Saturdays. This means that your advantage could be extended hours in the evening and being open on Saturdays to provide service to those in the community who don't do business at all because of the time conflict or those who would prefer to do it at a more convenient time for their schedules. Having the extended hours could potentially bring in new clients from the community and influence some of the other businesses' customers your way.

In identifying the competition in this case, it was determined that an aggressive marketing campaign before the doors even opened would be necessary and that not only should it identify the service but also what has been determined to be the business's competitive advantage, which will be extended hours during the week and Saturday hours.

Obviously, there will be different research completed for other types of companies. A tech start-up may find that its advantage is getting to the market first. An inventor might find he or she can produce a similar product currently in the market for cheaper, so he or she can price the new product cheaper when it enters the market. What will be consistent is that there will always be competition and that entrepreneurs need to identify and learn from their competition. If not, they may have already lost and just don't know it.

Session Review Question: What will be your competitive advantage?

COACHING SESSION 26

Who Is Your Customer?

> You just have to pay attention
> to what people need and
> what has not been done.
> —RUSSELL SIMMONS, FOUNDER
> OF DEF JAM RECORDS

There are a few questions that I ask any entrepreneur to help me grasp the size of the business and determine if I might know someone in my current network with whom I could connect this potential client. Surprisingly, there is one simple question that, about half of the time, many have a challenge with responding to. That question is, "Who is your *niche* customer?"

Now, you might be surprised to hear that an entrepreneur might not know who his or her niche customer is, or you might even be pondering yourself who that may be now or when you open your own business. With all the responsibilities of creating and running a new business, entrepreneurs can sometimes lose their way by focusing on developing the product or service and never identify who their niche customers are and what they might actually want. The end result for an aspiring entrepreneur is developing a business that is not really geared toward anyone; for an established business, it is having customers but not knowing how to market to others like them. Both of these situations can contribute to the failure of your business.

Most times, an aspiring entrepreneur should identify his or her niche customer in the business planning stage. This information can range from how many people live in the community to the average household income. Other times, a product will be launched for one customer base, and another might adopt it. Regardless of the stage of your business or product development, answering the following five questions will make sure you know who your niche client actually is.

1. **How many potential customers do I have access to?** Knowing this number will allow you to project how many people will actually need your service, and from there you can project if you can sell enough not only to stay in business but to also determine how much potential profit is out there. For instance, if you make one dollar on each sale, that means you "only" need one million sales to make your MDI come to reality. After completing your research, you determine that there are only two hundred thousand people who might buy your product. This does not

mean your dream of having an MDI is over; you just now need to figure out how to make five dollars on each sale.

2. **What age group prefers my service?** Knowing the age range of your customer provides a significant amount of information for your business. This information will allow you to better understand where and when to market your product, making sure that you get in front of those who have a higher propensity to buy it. Once you know the age range of your group, you will know how to connect and reconnect with it. This means instead of trying to connect with young adults across all the major social media platforms, for example, your best bet would be to put your energy into Instagram versus Pinterest. On the other hand, if your service is geared toward women thirty-five years and older, you have to be on Pinterest.

3. **Can my customers afford my product or service?** Just because you may want to charge a certain price for your product does not mean that it will be the price your customers will like. If your customer base is more affluent, then a high price might be warranted, as it may support the prestige of the purchase, but if they are more price conscious, they may never even consider doing business with you, as they can do it somewhere else for cheaper.

4. **When do my customers like to do business?** Many times, business owners set their business hours at

times that are convenient for them without considering who their customers are, and this can be a big mistake. A business might be open nine to five every day and closed on the weekend, but the niche customer typically works the same hours during the week and is only off on the weekends. This means the business's hours are the opposite of those of the customer base it built its services for needs, so how will they be able to do business with their customers?

5. **How often will they use your product or service?** Knowing the purchasing cycle of a customer base is a very important piece of information because it will determine how many opportunities you will have to do business. If you are a wedding planner, typically you will do business with a person once in a lifetime, which means you will always have to aggressively look out for new customers. If you are a barber whose client base comes in every two weeks, then your focus will need to be on making sure that they enjoy the experience and will come back over and over and over again.

Once they are able to answer these questions, most entrepreneurs will have a baseline understanding of who their niche customers will actually be or are currently. And with this knowledge, each will be able to design a business model that will help create the most possible interactions with customers by knowing what they need and the best way to market to them. An increase in customer interactions, be it through having more overall clients or just increasing the number and frequency of repeat customers, will lead to one thing for sure: more business. Now, it will be up to the entrepreneur to turn that business into profit.

Session Review Question: How do you know your product or service will attract and retain clients?

COACHING SESSION 27

A Great Product Is Not Enough!

> Don't be cocky. Don't be flashy. There
> is someone always better than you.
> —TONY HSIESH, CEO OF ZAPPOS

think everyone has heard a story about how a very successful entrepreneur went to bed one night and then woke up the next morning with the best idea for a product or service ever! The entrepreneur then took this idea and went on to have unimaginable success overnight. These are always great stories to hear, and I will not debate that waking up with great ideas in the morning is not possible. I am actually a firm believer in that and encourage my clients to write their thoughts down first thing in the morning. The problem that I have with this story is the second part: the idea that a great idea leads to overnight success. It discounts all the other work that needs to be done in most cases for an idea to go from a great thought to a great product or service and then become a great business. Many aspiring entrepreneurs think their success is a flip of the switch once they have a great idea and forget to ask themselves the following questions.

1. **How will people find out about my product?** Answering this question is key. I have spoken to many clients who spend so much time and energy on building out their product or service that they forget to market their business. Their belief is that once people use their product, they will automatically come back. Unfortunately, this is not true in the majority of the cases. And if they do come back, will their return business be consistent or of a sporadic nature? It is crucial, especially at the beginning, for entrepreneurs to build sales momentum by aggressively marketing their product to make sure people know that they actually have a product and why theirs is better than or different from the competition's.

2. **Will I provide a quality product every time?** There is a great quote that goes, "You only have one time to make a first impression." This is especially true in the business world, where word-of-mouth advertising and repeat customers are crucial to profitability. As a new business launches, it has to focus on the quality of the product being at a high level, because every customer is a new customer. These customers will not care about the ramp-up time that is required; they expect quality day one. How many times have you gone to a restaurant for the first time, and the food you

ordered was subpar? The real question is: How many times have you gone back since?

3. **Will my customer service meet expectations?** Once your marketing kicks in and you get new customers, there will be a need to provide a level of customer service that they expect. A great customer service experience is not only the right thing to do for people who do business with you; it is also the only way to do business if you expect those customers to come back or for them to refer others to you. For instance, let's say that a new coffee shop opens, and it advertises a very special blend of coffee that people actually want to try. It is so popular that it sells out fast in the morning, so no one who comes after nine is able to get the special blend. Instead of blending more coffee or advertising it for a special time only, customers are just told, "We are out." This lack of meeting customer expectations leads to the reputation of being the new coffee shop that runs out of coffee and a higher likelihood new customers will also say, "We are out," and business will decline.

Great new products are launched every day, and great new businesses close every day. Becoming aware that a great product is only one piece of the puzzle to running your business will ensure that yours is not one of those that will be closing.

Session Review Question: Other than having a great product or service, what else about your business will attract customers?

COACHING SESSION 28

Test Your Market!

> What do you need to start a business?
> Three simple things: know your product
> better than anyone. Know your customer,
> and have a burning desire to succeed.
> —DAVE THOMAS, FOUNDER OF WENDY'S

A lot of times, entrepreneurs get the idea to build a business based on something they love to do or a need they have. There is a great quote that states, "Necessity is the mother of invention," which supports this philosophy. Necessity has truly led to some of the greatest inventions and millions of successful businesses. This is because these entrepreneurs filled the need of the market. Sometimes, the need of the market is evident, and other times, it might be a shot in the dark. Either way, it's beneficial to test the market before any business is launched.

Years ago, I had the opportunity to facilitate focus groups, and it opened my eyes to how much corporations invest in doing market research before they launch any product. One of my groups focused simply on how customers perceived the company and how likely they would be to do business with them in the future if the company launched a new product they had in mind. The overall opinion was that a good majority of the participants felt that they would not be able to afford the product from the company, so they doubted they would purchase it. The company did not scrap the idea but realized they had a branding problem that they had to manage when they launched the new product. If companies worth billions of dollars see value in testing the market, then there is some value in any aspiring business owner doing so as well. As I work with my clients, I always encourage them to test the market before they launch because at the end of the day, the product or service has to meet your customers' needs to actually sell. Just because you love something does not mean others will love it as much as you do or even at all.

One of the easiest ways to test the market is to create your own focus group. You will not have the budget of a Fortune 500 company, but you should be able to find people similar to the market you think would be interested and simply ask them. These people can be family, friends, or associates, and as long as you feel they fit the description of someone in your market, their feedback will be beneficial. Obtaining feedback can be accomplished in a group setting over dinner or a conference call, or it could be as simple as an e-mail poll. For those who say it is hard to find people to discuss it with, my question is: "If it is hard to find them now, how hard will it be to find them when the business actually opens?"

Sometimes it is easier to determine if the product or service will sell, as there will be other businesses in the market similar to your plan. If there are similar businesses, it means there is a market, but it also means there will be competition. In these cases, testing your market is easy. It can be as easy as "shopping" your future competition. For instance, if the plan is to open a restaurant in a certain area, it would be beneficial to visit some of the restaurants in the local area to determine the type of food sold, the menu prices, and the level of customer service. This research will go a long way in determining how well a new restaurant would fit in the area. It would show what services and prices customers are accustomed to. Also, this would help in determining how much may need to be spent on advertising and marketing. Going back to the example, if the restaurant idea is to offer Italian cuisine and there are already two established Italian restaurants in the market, then it will cost to attract customers away from those other locations. Not that competition is bad, nor should it deter you from opening the business, but in many cases, it will make it more expensive to be profitable, and that is something that you need to plan for before you open.

Another, more involved way to test the market is something that is called a *soft launch,* meaning that you invest enough time and resources to actually create a product or service before launching full scale to determine what will work and what might not work as well. In the restaurant industry, a great example of this is the popularity of food trucks. Many chefs who aspire to open restaurants are now starting with food trucks first, as the cost is cheaper, ranging on average between $50,000 and $80,000 compared to opening a physical location that will range between $100,000 and $300,000. Here, they can test different items to see how interested people will be in the menu and, in some cases, find out where the restaurant should actually be located. Now, that option may still sound expensive for some, but there are additional opportunities to have a soft launch, depending on your business model.

Testing your market will confirm you are on to a great product already or that you need to tweak it to what your customers prefer; in some cases, you might find that there is not enough of a market to have the success you thought you might. Either way, wouldn't it be easier to ask the market what it wants before it tells you?

Session Review Question: What is the market currently telling you about the need for your product or service?

Entrepreneur's Reality Check:
"Everyone has stones thrown their way. Some throw them back, but others use them to build an EMPIRE."

- Roddric W. Sims
www.SimsCoachingGroup.com

Section Three Takeaways: Environment

What quote will you share?

_____

_____

_____

Whom will you share it with?

_____

Which coaching session resonated with you the most? And why?

_____

_____

_____

_____

_____

What was your biggest takeaway from this section?

_____

_____

_____

_____

What three actions are you ready to take now based on what you've learned? And by when?

1. _____ Date: _____
2. _____ Date: _____
3. _____ Date: _____

Who will be your accountability partner?

_____

What does success look like when you have accomplished your goals?

_____
_____
_____
_____
_____

What will you do to celebrate when these goals have been accomplished?

_____
_____
_____

Section Four

The 4th E of Entrepreneurship—Execution

Execution[6]

- the act of doing or performing something

---

6 *Merriam-Webster*, s.v. "Execution," accessed July 10, 2016, http://www.merriam-webster.com/dictionary/execution.

COACHING SESSION 29

Making Time to Succeed

> Focus on being productive
> instead of busy.
> — TIMOTHY FERRISS, AUTHOR
> OF *THE 4-HOUR WORKWEEK*

As I meet new people and they find out that I coach entrepreneurs, the conversation eventually leads to the great idea they had that someone else has launched. Ironically, I feel their pain, as I have a few of those too! The biggest difference I find between people who succeed with their ideas and those who don't is basically those who succeed actually execute on those ideas. It sounds pretty simple, but it is definitely true. Simply taking action magnifies your probability of success exponentially.

Naturally, during these conversations, my questions lead to why they didn't take action. The majority of the time, the response is, "I was just too busy with other things" or "I couldn't find the time." I won't debate the legitimacy of those responses but instead will focus on three steps to make time to succeed or execute on that great idea.

1. **Prioritize.** There will always be too many things to do. That's just the way it is for successful people. In order to manage it all, you have to prioritize what is important to you. For example, is the two hours of television, surfing the Internet, or stopping by the bar more important than working on that business idea? If the answer is "no," then we may have already found you some time to work on that great idea. I have had sessions with clients who have deferred going back get their MBA because their business ideas were a higher priority at that time. If they can make that sacrifice, I am sure giving up a little TV time should be feasible for the masses.

2. **Set time to work for yourself.** For those who have another job, finding time to execute on that great idea is definitely a challenge that cannot be wished away, especially since you might need that income to support you and your family. I encourage my clients to find time—let me change that to *make* time—to work for themselves. So, if you put in forty to fifty hours a week at your job, how do you find more time? Well, we already touched on that with the first point, which was "prioritize." Now that you have found the time, make sure you know how many hours you can work

for yourself a week. The range I see from most clients realistically tends to be between ten and twenty hours a week.

3. **Make it a routine.** Now that you have prioritized your time and figured out how many hours you can work for yourself, you now have to create a routine that will allow you to be consistent—just like a normal workday with set hours, you should do the same to work on your idea. Being consistent will not only establish a new entrepreneurial mind-set but also allow you to better manage all of the other responsibilities you have. You can now schedule them around your work time or schedule your work time around them.

Once you make time to succeed, you can take advantage of those great ideas. The law of averages shows us that not all of them will work, but as we see daily, it only takes executing on one great idea to change your life.

Session Review Question: How often do you make time to work on your business rather than working in your or someone else's business?

COACHING SESSION 30

How to Align Your Passion with Your Business Idea

> A business that makes nothing
> but money is a poor business.
> —HENRY FORD, FOUNDER OF
> FORD MOTOR COMPANY

Many times I am asked, "Should I start a business focused on something that I am passionate about?" My answer is, "Maybe, but it depends on if you plan to make this a business or a hobby." There are several reasons for this statement because opening a business is so much more than working in your passion. Many times, people are passionate about their hobbies because the hobbies take them away from the normal stresses of life. Typically, the more successful your business becomes, the less time you spend doing what you are passionate about. And instead of reducing stress, running the business can increase it exponentially.

Let's say you love making widgets and decided you want open up the Widget Store. You go through all the red tape of opening your business, and you launch your store in a great location. Things start out well, and your business is making money, but you feel that something is off. "Why?" you may ask. Well, let's take a look at a few things.

First, instead of working eight hours a day and five days a week at your old job, you are now working ten to twelve hours a day and six days a week. Your store is only open from nine to five, but you have to be there a couple of hours beforehand to get the store ready for business in the morning, and then you have to stay after the store closes to make the widgets for the next day. Plus, now you have to go into the office every Saturday when you were typically off. You are spending more time working.

Second, in order to run the Widget Store, you need to hire, train, and manage employees. You notice that these responsibilities take a third of your time now…much less time to make those widgets than you thought.

Finally, even though the Widget Store is generating cash, you notice that you spend a lot of what you make by putting it back into your business. You pay your business loans, the materials to make the widgets, salary for employees, and so on. You do get what's left over, but it is not as much as the salary from your last job and the amount varies from week to week.

You have gone from loving to make widgets to having the Widget Store potentially becoming the biggest factor for stress in your life. Now, when you think about making widgets, it is no longer a hobby or even fun!

If you want to run a business but still stay passionate about your hobby, consider finding a business or job that you won't mind running. This will allow you to have more time for your hobby, not less time, which running the Widget Store could cause.

Here are a few suggestions to help you find the appropriate way to align your passion with your business:

1. Decide if it is more important to have more time or more control over your time. There is a big difference! Your business may not allow you to be off every weekend, but it could allow you to pick your child up from school every day or volunteer your time for a charity.

2. Determine if you want to manage people. Even though there tends to be a direct correlation between the number of people employed in a business and the income potential, driving results through others is a responsibility that some people would rather not deal with at a large level. There are many opportunities that allow you to be a "solopreneur," which means you only have to manage one employee, yourself.

3. Check to make sure that your hobby is something that you want to do and think about every day. When you do something once a month or once a week, it stays fresh and provides you with something to look forward to. In contrast, when

you have to work in it every day, you may have to find something else to replace it.

Session Review Questions: What part of your business are you most passionate about and why?

COACHING SESSION 31

Things Successful Entrepreneurs Need to Do Every Day!

> I don't look to jump over seven-foot bars—I look for one-foot bars that I can step over.
> —WARREN BUFFETT, CHAIRMAN AND CEO OF BERKSHIRE HATHAWAY

A successful experience as an entrepreneur is not a random occurrence. One of the most important assets entrepreneurs possess is their time. It takes daily intentional and deliberate acts to make sure that they are making the most of it.

As you venture off into your journey as an entrepreneur, you need to make sure you use the time you have wisely, so here are four things you can do every day that will make sure you are on the path to success:

1. **Plan your day.** Most entrepreneurs go to bed thinking about their businesses and wake up working on them. In order to make the most of this, you should make a list of your top priorities and plan your day around completing the most important tasks first. If you do not, you can spend your day doing a bunch of work, but sometimes it can just be busywork and not work that is going to make your business actually work.

2. **Focus on one thing at a time.** In today's world, there are many distractions, and when you add in the varying responsibilities of an entrepreneur, you will feel the pressure of doing multiple tasks at once. Don't do it! Research shows that even though you might feel as though you are accomplishing more, the mistakes that you make and the double work that takes place will diminish your long-term outcomes. With so many responsibilities, being efficient is the key to your success.

3. **Keep your vision at the forefront.** The vision you design for your business should be something you review daily. When you created it, it was to place your ideas and goals into one place. By reviewing this vision, you will make sure that every action you take aligns with the direction you would like to take your business. If you do not, you may go too far down the path to someone else's vision and create the wrong business.

4. **Learn how to delegate.** As a new entrepreneur, your initial instinct is to try to do everything all the time. You should always look for ways to free up your time to do the important work in your business. As you are doing tasks, you should ask yourself, "Could someone else do this for me?" Initially, because of finances, it may not be realistic for you to delegate, but as you continue to fulfill the vision of your business and grow, there will come a time when you trying to do everything will begin to stunt the growth of your business. When that happens, the list of items you can delegate will come in handy.

There is always a financial conversation held with any business owner about getting the proper return on financial investments. It is my opinion that the ROI on how you use your time is even more important. As you grow your business, you can always ask for more investment capital to cover early mistakes, but you will never be able to get wasted time back.

Session Review Question: What is the one thing you can change about your daily routine that will give your business the biggest boost?

COACHING SESSION 32

All Aspiring Entrepreneurs Should Have a Game Plan

> See things in the present, even
> if they are in the future.
> —LARRY ELLISON, COFOUNDER
> OF ORACLE CORPORATION

The majority of the clients I coach are already employed full-time prior to them even considering owning their own businesses. The challenges that they face in making a smooth transition from being an employee to actually running their own businesses come at them in many ways. They spend a significant amount of time game planning for the big day when they are in a position to open their own businesses. If you are considering a move into the world of entrepreneurship, here are a few tips to follow as you develop your own game plan.

1. **Plan early.** If you can identify and start working on your business eighteen to twenty-four months in advance of launch, this will help you significantly. You will hear a lot of advice that will recommend you open your business as soon as possible. There are a lot of reasons that this makes sense. For instance, if you are in the tech world, being first to market can be a competitive advantage from a branding and product-placement position. For the majority of entrepreneurs who are already entering a mature marketplace, it is better to do your research way in advance to determine who your competitors are and how your business can create its own niche.

2. **Shift your mind-set.** A key to becoming a successful entrepreneur is establishing the right mind-set. Changing your mind-set from that of an employee to that of a business owner can be a challenge for some. As an employee, you typically have a steady income, set work hours, and one specific role in the company. When you move to the world of entrepreneurship that will change substantially. The steady income becomes fluctuating income. You go from working a set forty hours a week to "until the job gets done." The role responsibilities also will get blurry, as you will in most cases be the manager, technical expert, and administrator every day. In some cases, your game plan will need to include shifting the mind-sets of your family and close friends. At the beginning of your business, you

may not have the ability to support them financially or emotionally as you may have in the past. This can lead to unexpected external pressures that can impact the focus you will need for your business.

3. **Start saving.** A significant number of businesses that fail do so for one reason, and that reason is lack of investment capital to provide cash flow. When your game plan includes how much capital you will need to start your business and what you will need monthly to pay all the bills, your chances for success increase exponentially. Identifying this information in advance will benefit you in many ways, but the most significant is that you will know how much money you will need to have on the front end; if you don't already have it, you will be able to adjust your current lifestyle and start saving.

Having a game plan may not guarantee you success as an entrepreneur, but it will provide an opportunity to prepare for some of the challenges you will face and increase your chances to stay in the game.

Session Review Question: How much time have you spent developing a game plan to create a successful business model?

COACHING SESSION 33

Get Off to a Strong Start as an Entrepreneur by Creating Value, Growth, and Connectivity

> Ideas are commodity.
> Execution of them is not.
> —MICHAEL DELL, FOUNDER
> AND CEO OF DELL

As you consider becoming an entrepreneur, know that marketing is an important skill for your business, as well as for your own personal brand. Anything can be marketed: a product, an idea, yourself, or your viewpoint. The biggest mistake people make is thinking that if they *just* get their name "out there," they're going to see results. The next biggest mistake is waiting until you open your doors and then starting marketing efforts. Marketing takes time, and there needs to be a ramp-up period to build momentum and buzz. But no matter what and when you're marketing, there are effective methods and ineffective methods. And while the type of marketing you do can depends a lot on your industry and business model, there are several important actions that are pretty much universal. Let's discuss the four that I believe are most crucial:

Start Early
If you wait until your business opens to start your marketing efforts, you are too late! Communication to your potential customer needs to start at least ninety days in advance of your launch, with the intent of creating a buzz. You want to have many customers day one, and normally it takes at least sixty days for a majority of marketing efforts to take off. Not many new businesses can afford to wait for sixty days or more before their targeted customer base realizes that they are even there.

Create Value
Instead of trying to capture customers by asking them to do something, try to form a lifelong customer by creating value. Many successful brands don't have a call to action in their message but instead have a clear demonstration of the value they bring to the market—which then creates action itself. In the long term, the more value you provide, the more customers will be willing to pay for *and* refer your services. Have you heard the term "referrals are gold"? Once the referrals start rolling in, make sure that you ask those customers to share the value you provide with their friends and families. If

this type of "word-of-mouth" marketing is done right, it can lead to exponential growth.

Focus on Growth

An organization that helps a client to grow will be a successful one. An audience's goal, regardless of age or socioeconomic status, is growth. In fact, everyone's main goal has an element of growing or learning in some way. Try marketing to your audience in a way that shows how your brand can help them achieve their desired outcomes. As your customer base grows, so can the products or services that you can offer them.

Connecting and Compelling Communication

Connecting with your audience is a must! Your message will most likely not compel people if they do not see any reason to read or share it. The audience will be more likely to retain the information and be more willing to take action if the communication is compelling. Try packaging ideas within a story to promote the audience's subconscious to relate to the idea being communicated. Make sure that the story being told is something that the audience can understand and relate to. If they are able to do both, you will be surprised that your customers will start telling your story as well.

When customers see the value of your service and you stay connected with them by providing opportunities for growth through timely marketing, your business will grow too. Now this is what I would call a "win-win" outcome.

Session Review Question: How will you know that the marketing for your business has gotten off to a strong start?

COACHING SESSION 34

Entrepreneurs Need to Be Prepared to Recover from the Unexpected

> When everything seems to be going
> against you, remember that the airplane
> takes off against the wind, not with it.
> —HENRY FORD, FOUNDER OF
> FORD MOTOR COMPANY

Being an entrepreneur is a huge responsibility, and you never really know what to expect. Some challenges are easy to see coming, such as finding trustworthy employees and building brand recognition. The real hurdles are the things you never planned on or predicted. They vary from business to business but take place in every new entrepreneurial endeavor.

There are a lot of unexpected events that can occur long after the doors close for the day, anything from a burglar alarm going off or an employee becoming sick to a flooding basement. An entrepreneur must be ready for unexpected events because they could ultimately be the downfall of the business. To help you prepare for these unexpected situations, consider having the following:

1. **Continuity plan**—Even though there is significant debate about how much information should go into your first business plan, there is no doubt that as your business grows, so should the plan. One of the crucial parts that needs to be added to any developed business plan is a "continuity plan." This plan basically covers what needs to be done in case there is an emergency or some interruption of your business. It will provide a plan and the information necessary for the business to stay open or get reopened as soon as possible. For instance, if your computer crashes, where will you have the important information backed up and whom should you call to help fix the computer? This same consideration should be given to other aspects of your business that could be damaged or stolen.

2. **Cash flow reserves**—Any business can have a bad week, month, or quarter that can significantly impact the business's cash flow. Surveys show that the number one reason why new business owners have to close their doors is because they have to spend more money than they are making; therefore, they might not be able to make their payroll, keep up with the rent, or do any additional marketing to attract new customers. Even after a

successful business gets past this point, its income will still typically fluctuate throughout the year. Having cash flow reserves already established will help manage those tight times. Since the hope is that you never have to use them, business lines of credit, open credit cards, or personal savings are usually the easiest way to set them up.

3. **Insurance**—No matter what the size of your business is, you should consider having business insurance. It is pretty obvious why when you consider the need to potentially replace property and the liability protection it provides in case you are sued, but I am surprised by how many people aren't aware that it also includes income replacement if your business is shut down because of a covered loss and, in some cases, if a *key employee* becomes incapacitated. It may sound like an expense, but it is actually an investment in the longevity of your business.

Just like in life, there is no way to avoid all the risks that take place in business. The best thing that you can do in most cases is expect the best but plan for the worst. You hope once you get these items in place, you never have to use them, but they will definitely let you and your business sleep well at night.

Session Review Question: How will you protect your business from disruptions?

COACHING SESSION 35

The Difference between Owning a Business and a "Busyness"

> The big secret in life is that there is no
> big secret. Whatever your goal, you can
> get there if you're willing to work.
> —Oprah Winfrey, founder
> of the OWN Network

Any aspiring entrepreneur will be called on to wear many hats when starting out in business. The challenge is to make sure that the efforts that are put forward are related to establishing and growing a business and not just being busy. It is easy to get caught up with a lot of things in the business that keep you busy but may not necessarily be income-producing activities. I have noticed during my thousands of hours coaching small business owners that there comes a time when a business plateaus because the owner no longer can focus on the vision. One of the main reasons is that the owner is too busy managing the day-to-day activities and no longer has time to focus on developing products or services to fit the needs of future clients. Here are a few tips to help you turn the busy time into business time.

1. **Set time aside to review your business plan.** Some of the most critical parts of any business plan are the vision and mission statements. The business owner should review these at least quarterly to make sure they are still in alignment with the owner's daily actions. After a review, an entrepreneur will know if his or her daily actions are in alignment with the vision and mission because they will be either closer or further away. If they are no closer, then there is a good chance that the entrepreneur is doing too much busywork or in other cases, the direction of the company may need to change. Without a regular review of the business plan, an opportunity to make the adjustments will never take place, and entrepreneurs will continue doing busy work and going in the wrong direction.

2. **Identify your income-producing activities (IPA).** One of the first things that the business owner needs to do is to determine his or her IPAs. The simple math shows us that the more time that is spent participating in activities that produce income, the more money that can actually be made. I know that this is not really earth-shattering news, but sometimes clarification of the

obvious is the best reinforcement. This will also allow you to determine the best way to spend your time and money.

3. **Delegate.** After you have identified those IPAs, it will be time to start delegating! This becomes a hard decision for many entrepreneurs because it is sometimes counterintuitive to why they started their businesses in the first place, which is really because they wanted more or total control. This becomes one of the cases where you have to give up some control in order to have more control. It will also allow you to manage your expenses much more efficiently. For instance, let's say you categorize your IPAs into categories, and two of the tasks make nine dollars per hour and some others make fifty dollars per hour. Knowing that you can't do everything, it probably makes more sense that the owner spends more time performing the tasks that generate fifty dollars per hour than those that make nine.

In my experience, the clients who have successfully followed these tips have a much better grasp of how important their time is and are able to make sure that their busy time is more about building their businesses rather than just being busy.

Session Review Question: What are your five most profitable income-producing activities (IPAs)?

COACHING SESSION 36

Entrepreneurship Is Not about Work-Life Balance; It Is about Work-Life Integration

> Early to bed, early to rise, work
> like hell and advertise.
> —TED TURNER, FOUNDER OF THE
> CABLE NEWS NETWORK (CNN)

Many of the clients I have worked with have had a significant amount of experience in corporate America, which has allowed them to gain invaluable experience to help them start and run their own businesses. Some of those skills are being results driven, process focused, and committed to high levels of customer service. Another concept that these clients bring with them is the theory of work-life balance. The theory of work-life balance is the idea that there is a need to separate your work from your personal life, as it can begin to impact your relationships, health, and state of mind in a negative way. Those who are committed to their careers can easily work sixty plus hours every week, travel for business a lot, and rarely if ever take vacation. Focusing on work-life balance equates to living a better quality of life. I am definitely a proponent of work-life balance in a person's career, but for entrepreneurs, I do not believe it is a realistic concept. I consider entrepreneurship to be more about work-life integration.

Work-life integration is about running your business and making it a part of your life. In an earlier coaching session, I shared with you the concept of starting a business being similar to raising a child. When you have a child, you have to adjust everything around you in order to take care of him or her. And most of the time, it is done by instinct. As an entrepreneur, you have to be willing to do just the same with your business. Your business has to have attention around the clock and needs to be part of your daily routine. Here are a few examples of how work-life integration plays out:

1. returning a key customer's call late at night when the customer is available
2. closing a deal over dinner
3. working on that business plan over the weekend
4. intentionally attending social events where potential customers will be
5. turning that extra bedroom into a home office
6. adding more entrepreneurs to your network of friends
7. business articles and books becoming part of your normal reading list

8. being always ready, willing, and able to talk about the business

9. keeping your personal and business schedule on the same calendar

In a career, you will have normal work hours, as your responsibility will only be for a portion of the business, but in the beginning as an entrepreneur, many times you are responsible for all of the business. There will not be a second shift to come in to finish the work that you began, nor will there be someone else you can delegate the work to when you go on vacation. Depending on how you structure your business if you are not able to do the work, then it will not get done.

As a business owner, your ability to integrate work into your life can actually have huge advantages. Since you are your own boss, you make your own work hours and have the flexibility to work whenever you want. So, if you want to pick your child up from school every day and then go back to work afterward, you can. If you want to volunteer some of your time during the workday without having your boss looking over your shoulder, you can. Or if you just want to work from home in your underwear, you can.

Focusing on work-life balance in your career allows you to live a better quality of life, but for entrepreneurs, focusing on work-life integration allows you to create a better quality of life.

Session Review Question: What are some of the opportunities that you have to integrate your personal and entrepreneurial life?

COACHING SESSION 37

Actions Solo Entrepreneurs Need to Take in Order to Maintain Their Sanity

> Genius is 1 percent inspiration,
> and 99 percent perspiration.
> —THOMAS EDISON, FOUNDER OF
> GENERAL ELECTRIC (GE)

A solopreneur is an entrepreneur who has one employee: him- or herself. And since a significant number of my clients are this type and most entrepreneurs, regardless of their business's size, tend to start out solo, I had to provide some insight here as well. This type of entrepreneur is "a one-person band," so the ability to balance time and prioritize is crucial. In order to keep these items and growth of the business at the forefront, there are three actions that every solopreneur needs to take.

1. **Treat your business like a business, not a hobby!**
   A significant amount of solopreneurs run their

businesses like a hobby. Most people work on their hobbies when they feel like it, but in business, this leads to inconsistency for the clients and the need of the services. Even though it is only you, your clients should not get that feeling in your interactions. Avoid the perception that you only work when you feel like it by setting weekly office hours so that clients know when you will be available. Make sure you stay focused on growing and developing your business by committing to a certain number of hours that you will work on it at a minimum weekly. Also, setting up separate telephone numbers and e-mail addresses for your business is a must, as you want to be able to separate your business communications from your personal communications about your hobbies.

2. **Schedule time to stay on plan.** As you operate as a solopreneur, you will be pulled in many directions at once. This is the nature of any entrepreneurial endeavor, so avoiding this challenge is not realistic, but what you can do is not let it get you off plan. Many times, you can be caught up in the day-to-day operations and lose track of the direction of your business. At a minimum, a monthly review of the progress that you are making toward your business plan goals is necessary. This will keep you moving in the right direction or allow you to make the necessary course corrections sooner rather than later. The further you get off plan, the harder it is to get back there,

so avoid getting of track altogether. Staying on plan!

3. **Create a support team.** When most solopreneurs start out, they feel as though they have to do everything from logo design to accounting. This is not the truth. Even though there may be some limitations on what can be outsourced to others based on investment capital and the proprietary nature of your products and services, you will still need a team to help you make the most of your time. A lot of entrepreneurs get so caught up in the day-to-day tactical activities of working in the business that they forget that it is as important to work on the strategic vision of the business. Having a team to help you will free up time for the strategic part and allow you to work on your business. This can be accomplished by adding a virtual assistant to help with the administrative items, a social media manager to handle your online brand, or crowdsourcing your logo design. Your team structure may be different, but you will have to have one to really maximize your opportunity.

Keeping these three things in mind may not guarantee success, but they will definitely help solopreneurs to maintain their sanity and focus.

Session Review Question: How long will you be able to run your business by yourself?

Entrepreneur's Reality Check:
"A GREAT plan without GREAT execution is a GREAT waste of time!"

– Roddric W. Sims
www.SimsCoachingGroup.com

Section Four Takeaways: Execution

What quote will you share?

_____
_____
_____

Whom will you share it with?

_____

Which coaching session resonated with you the most? And why?

_____
_____
_____
_____
_____

What was your biggest takeaway from this section?

_____
_____
_____
_____

What three actions are you ready to take now based on what you've learned? And by when?

1. _____ Date: _____
2. _____ Date: _____
3. _____ Date: _____

Who will be your accountability partner?

_____

What does success look like when you have accomplished your goals?

_____
_____
_____
_____
_____

What will you do to celebrate when these goals have been accomplished?

_____
_____
_____

CONCLUSION

I n my experience working with entrepreneurs, I have come to realize some of their most valuable resources are their time and money. So I truly appreciate you investing both in purchasing and taking the time to read *The Four Es of Entrepreneurship*. For those of you who are aspiring entrepreneurs, I hope I have provided you some perspective to help you clarify what you will need to do to be successful on your entrepreneurial adventure. For those who are already fully immersed in the world of entrepreneurship and may be on your second or third business, my intent was to reinforce things you may already know or bring to light some things that you might be trying to ignore.

You now know why exposure, understanding the economics, doing the proper research on the environment, and committing to execution are all key components to setting yourself up for success as an entrepreneur. You have also identified your takeaways from the coaching sessions, created an action plan, and identified your accountability partner(s). My coaching sessions and the failure rate of new businesses convince me you are now in better position than at least 50 percent of the people who start a new business because of the shift in your mind-set.

As a professional coach, my intent is always to move people toward actions that lead to the success that they aspire for. This book is only one of the ways that I plan to continue down that path. I would love to continue supporting you by asking you to visit my website and provide feedback on this book at *The Entrepreneur's Reality Coach Blog* or to connect with me on Twitter, Facebook, or Instagram. I also would love to connect just to follow your success as you grow your business because, as a coach, I win when you win.

So again: Ready! Set! Let's go!

Roddric W. Sims
Certified Coach - Entrepreneurship
Sims Coaching Group
Website: http://www.SimsCoachingGroup.com
E-mail: Roddric@SimsCoachingGroup.com
Twitter: @BizRealityCoach
Instagram: @BizRealityCoach

ABOUT THE AUTHOR

Roddric W. Sims specializes in working with highly motivated entrepreneurs and small business owners. His goals are to maximize their potential by helping them identify and overcome roadblocks to their personal and professional success. He has fondly been dubbed as the "Reality Coach" by his clients due to his pragmatic and direct approach to getting to the core of their problems, helping them set realistic goals and holding them accountable to their action plans. Sims proudly states, "Not only do I help my clients define success, I help them find success."

Over his 20 year professional career he has worked in varying roles related to sales, customer service, management and recruiting for a Fortune 50 company. During the last 10 years he has had the opportunity to coach over 2,000 aspiring entrepreneurs in group and one on one sessions with topics including, but not limited to business plan development, personal branding and interview skills. Roddric is also the founder of the Sims Coaching Group, LLC which is a coaching network that provides group coaching and workshops focused on entrepreneurship, career progression and leadership development.

Sims is a graduate of the University of Illinois – Chicago where he obtained a Bachelor's degree in Psychology. He has obtained the designation of Certified Coach through the Coach Training Alliance (CTA). He also currently holds the following professional designations: Chartered Property Casualty Underwriter (CPCU), Associate in Management (AIM), Associate in Claims (AIC) and Associate in Insurance Services (AIS). He is a member of the International Coaching Federation (ICF), Alpha Phi Alpha Fraternity, Inc., The 100 Black Men of Chicago and the Black Life Coaches Network.

Sims has two sons and lives in Chicago, Illinois.